Soccer's Principles of Play

Peter Prickett

DARK
RIVER

First published 2021 by Dark River

6 Woodside, Churnet View Road, Oakamoor, ST10 3AE, UK

ISBN: 9781911121923

ACKNOWLEDGEMENTS

Thank you to the people who have helped me write this book.

It started with a question I was asked by a Twitter user; they may not even remember asking the question. Why Mladen Jovanovic chose to ask me the question, I do not know, but if he hadn't this book wouldn't exist. He asked if there were any fundamentals of soccer he should be aware of. After some thinking, my answer was the Principles of Play.

He then asked, "Is there a book you can recommend?"

I couldn't. I could not think of a single book that focused on the general principles of soccer, rather than the specific principles of certain coaches. That was the birth of this book. Thank you, Mladen.

Thank you Garth Smith, for your excellent work on the cover, the third time I have asked you to design a book cover and the third time you have nailed it.

Thank you Dan Sheahan, for collaborating on the diagrams in the final chapter, transforming my diagrams from adequate into striking images.

A general thank you to those people with whom I discussed the ideas, asked to read chapters, and who offered advice during the writing process. You were all a huge help.

Finally, thank you, the reader, for supporting this book.

CONTENTS

Introduction

But only sometimes.

Soccer is a complex game, but it need not be complicated. Bill Shankly and Johan Cruyff have informed us well on this subject. The complexity comes from the huge number of possibilities within the game, plus the factor that there are relatively few rules (or laws).

By and large, these laws are in reference to equipment, officiating, and restarts. There are very few laws that impact the way in which the game is played. Indeed, the laws relating to handball, the goalkeeper, and offside, have the most influence on match play.

The most important law, however, is Law 10. *Determining the match.*

In order to find the heart of any matter – whether that be economics, justice, or soccer – we need to simplify. Possibly even to the point where the simplification is *extraordinarily* simple.

As fans and coaches, we enjoy a deep dive into the machinations of soccer. We immerse ourselves as one action triggers another, in a never-ending flow of perceptions and actions until the game is over.

Soccer is ultimately a finite game, though. A game that is played to win within a certain period, be that period the match itself or a competition. People become fixated upon studying the methods used by winning teams, but Law 10 tells us that there is only one way to win a match within the allotted time, and without utilizing additional mechanisms.

The team scoring the greater number of goals is the winner. If both teams score no goals or an equal number of goals, the match is drawn.

There sits Law 10, as written by the International Football Association Board.

Strip everything back. Remove opinions and preferences. Take away the influences of the individuals. Score more goals than the other team, in whatever numerical combination you care to conceive. Failure to do so is a failure to win. It is a failure to understand the heart of the matter.

Principles are fundamental and universal truths. If we take language, the primary principle is that children first learn what they hear most. In a democracy, a key principle is that of popular sovereignty; the idea that the people are the ultimate authority of government. The major religions share the principles of community, group cohesion, and identity. It is possible that there are multiple universal truths, but it is vital to understand *which* principles are universal and which are personal, becoming more akin to ideals.

The fashion in coaching is to study the playing philosophy of successful teams. Generally, this will be with a particular focus on the coaches of that day, while also paying due attention to those who came before. The word 'philosophy' is often used very freely and loosely, with little relation to the *wider term philosophy*. What is really being looked at is a set of beliefs, values, and ideals that formulate a game model, equating to a *playing style*.

Genuine philosophical branches such as ontology and epistemology do influence soccer. Ontology studies the nature of being and the relationship between concepts. Epistemology studies knowledge, with particular attention on methods, validity, and scope. Through ontology and epistemology, we may discover a set of truths for the playing of the game of soccer.

Thousands of pages have been dedicated to the systems of Guardiola, Klopp, Mourinho, and others. And in the principles that they use. I cautiously use the word principle here, as I am wary of confusion. A coach can have their own principles, but these principles may not necessarily be the universal principles (even though the coach's personal principles may be born of the universal principles).

Guardiola is closely associated with the tiki-taka style (however much he dislikes the term). A broad description would be that this method of play is position-based, possession-based, and seeks to dominate the opposition. Does that make these points the principles of play? They may be for Guardiola, but they are not universally true. Claudio Ranieri's Leicester City were champions without seeking to dominate possession of the ball.

Jurgen Klopp is associated with counter-pressing – regaining the ball as close to the opposition goal as possible – even claiming that counter-pressing creates more chances than any playmaker. Is this personal principle a universal principle? Regaining the ball in some form is likely to be a universal goal for any soccer team, but where the regain happens can be very different.

 It's absolutely normal that different human beings want to go different ways.

Jurgen Klopp

Almost every coach will have their idea of how they think soccer should be played. It is possible to have completely different ideas of what professional soccer should look like, and for those opposing views to both yield success. Arguably, this is what has made the clashes between Jose Mourinho and Pep Guardiola so fascinating. Neither was right or wrong; they were just different – based on their personal principles, ideals, and values.

There is a huge difference between the personal principles at play in the professional game, and any personal principles at play in youth soccer.

In the professional game, it is the job of Guardiola, Klopp, Mourinho *et al.* to win. In youth soccer, that is not necessarily the job of the coach. It is the job of the coach to engage, educate, enlighten, and make playing enjoyable (amongst other jobs). The personal ideals of a brand of soccer – or what a coach believes will win soccer matches – is unlikely to be important to the young players. Asking 9-year-olds to play a short, fast, patient passing style, where we move the ball to move the opposition, might look incredible but might also produce a limited picture for those youngsters. As might asking them to sit in a deep defensive block and then spring counter-attacks!

I am personally convinced that, in adult soccer, it is quite easy to win between 35% and 45% of your games. If you defend quite deep with a back four, and a line of three midfielders in front of the back four, leaving two very fast forwards in wide positions where the opposition fullbacks should be, with no center-forward, but an attack-minded midfield – the team will catch most sides on the break often enough to win. It will not always be good to watch, but that raw pace in high and wide areas will work. Is this my personal principle? No. It does not match with my ideology and values. This is *not* the way I would like to see soccer played. Is this idea based on the principles of play? Yes, it certainly is.

Soccer does not exist in isolation. It is an invasion game and exists within a family of related games, with related outcomes. Rugby's laws about passing are distinct from soccer, and Netball's laws about movement and ball carrying are distinct from soccer, yet both games involve scoring on (or in) some form of target. This is a commonality amongst invasion games – a truth beyond specific sports.

By having an understanding of the principles of play, we can form tactics and game understanding through which players can unlock effective decision-making in-game. By stripping soccer back to the universal principles of play, and removing personal principles or preferences, we should be able to obtain clarity and look into the fundamentals of soccer.

In this book, I seek to address the universal truth(s) of soccer. What are the principles of play in soccer? What role do these principles have in our practice design?

Once we understand the principles of play, can we then build a philosophy based on truths of the game, or use our understanding of the truths to build a better understanding of game models and why they exist?

Let's find out.

Principles of Invasion Games

Soccer is indeed a part of a family of games; but, more specifically, it is a part of a family of *invasion* games – games constructed around the concepts of attack, defense, and scoring. In order to be most successful, we need to invade our opponent's territory.

The core objective of invasion games is to move the ball into an opponent's territory in order to score. To achieve this objective, the players must maintain possession of the ball, create and use space, and attack a goal.

Werner, Thorpe, and Bunker

Werner, Thorpe, and Bunker were key protagonists in the development of the 'teaching games for understanding' methodology, a widely utilized approach in coaching. Their summary of invasion games further illustrates that soccer is not isolated; the game has a great many cousins that share important properties with soccer. Before embracing the principles of soccer, it would be prudent to examine the principles of other family members, for surely no truth could be more universal than if it transcends multiple sports?

There are two possible barriers to this idea. The rules of the game may disqualify certain principles, or the rules of the game may mean that certain principles emerge in a unique manner in certain games. The second barrier, in turn, may be the language used to describe the principles, requiring us to draw conclusions with regard to how the principles transfer between sports, if they transfer at all.

Hockey is a good example here. It's a sport that has sought to simplify its principles, stripping the game back to a bare few.

In-possession	Out-of-possession	In-possession – Transition – Out-of-possession
Move the ball to go forward – Carry to go forward – Take the best option to go forward	Apply pressure on receivers – Defensive skills on the move – Win the ball back – Stop their go forward	Score points
Goal scoring	Keep them under pressure	Go forward
		Provide support
		Create continuity
		Apply pressure
		Contest possession

Away from Hockey, Rugby might (at first) appear more complex, due to the players' inability to pass the ball forward with the hands. However, if we consider that Hockey uses the phrase "Take the best option to go forward", that will also apply to rugby, with those options being to carry the ball or kick.

Netball has a similar issue to Rugby, in that dribbling or carrying the ball is not allowed. This means that the "Best option to go forward" is always going to be a pass.

In-possession	Out-of-possession
Attack and gain the front position on a defender	Delay the attacker moving through the court to goal
Maintain-possession and move the ball into open space	Force errors
Identify space or gaps in the defense	Close down space
Use a variety of setups for a successful center pass	Force errors at the center pass
Select the most appropriate pass into the circle to score goals	Reduce available options

Basketball is possibly more like Soccer than Rugby and Netball as it has more variations on progressing forward, with both dribbling and forward passing allowed. The principles are more in-depth and more numerous.

In-possession	Defensive transition	Out-of-possession	Offensive transition
Getting open	Rebounding	Disrupt ball movement	Rebounding and outletting
Spacing	Protecting the basket	Stop penetrating moves	Progression up the court
Ball circulation	Slowing/stopping ball progression	Helping and rotating	Exploit numerical advantages
Penetrating the defense	Defending numerical disadvantages	Defending special situations	Exploit spatial advantages
Extending the advantage	Defending spatial disadvantages	Rebounding	Transitioning to half-court offence
Shot selection			

We can see that certain principles have striking similarities. The principles of going forward or penetration exists in all games, even if the method is different.

Conversely, delaying or stopping the forward movement is also evident. Applying pressure seems to permeate across the games. Supporting and helping teammates in attack and defense crosses over the games. In effect, there is a need to utilize and protect spaces. No matter what the scoring system or laws of the game, these principles seem to apply.

At this point, it is important to note that it was through Allen Wade's 1968 book – The FA Guide to Training and Coaching – that the idea of principles of play became concrete. Within this book, Wade outlined five principles of attack and defense; other sports have taken from these original principles.

Attack	Defense
Penetration	Delay
Support	Depth
Width	Concentration (compaction)
Mobility	Balance
Improvisation/Creativity	Discipline/Patience

Over time, the principles have had slight modifications in soccer, as well as other sports, with the element of *transition* gaining prominence. However, it is these core principles that have been taught to coaches by the English Football Association across the decades.

For many years, these principles of play have been largely unchallenged. However, although these are the principles of play taught by the English Football Association, they do not represent the entirety of principles being taught by other national governing bodies. Therefore, we cannot surmise that these principles are exhaustive, though we might consider them to be a good starting point.

If we review the common threads between sports, the principle of penetration or "go forward" is prominent. Werner, Thorpe, and Bunker allude to this with their closing sentiment of "attack a goal". Connecting this to the laws of most invasion games – with regards to deciding the outcome – it is plausible to make a case that the only *true principle* is to score. For higher-scoring sports (e.g., Basketball), expressing scoring as a principle could be realistic, but for lower-scoring sports (e.g., Soccer), setting scoring as a principle in itself may be too unrealistic.

Soccer is the lowest-scoring of mainstream invasion games, which may explain why scoring was not included in Allen Wade's original principles of play. A more realistic principle might be to look for the chance to score. In Netball, that has to be close to the scoring circle; the laws dictate this. In Rugby, the scoring of a try must be beyond the try line. In Rugby, it is theoretically possible to kick points from anywhere on the field, but the reality is the closer we are to the posts, the more chance we have of scoring. The same is true of Basketball, Hockey and Soccer. Hence, the idea of invading territory makes it easier to score, and the principle of penetration or "go forward" is the key principle when in-possession. Inversely, preventing the opposition from going forward becomes the key out-of-possession principle. How these things are achieved will link to the other principles of play.

In-possession, principles of support, width, mobility, and improvisation/creativity may help a team to score, but it cannot be definitely said that all of these principles are absolutely necessary in any given moment in order to score.

The defending principles generally exist in closer unison, but can be more open to interpretation. For instance, there are various ways in which teams can choose to set up their defensive depth – with lines of engagement and defensive lines closer or further from the goal, depending on strategy. No method is right, but in Soccer, this principle is impacted by the offside law, which creates a natural reference point for defensive depth. Principles can be applied in differing and inventive ways.

Coaching methodologies have also developed the principles of play into a cycle.

While the cycle has not been widely used for as long as the principles of play, it has also gone largely unchallenged until recently.

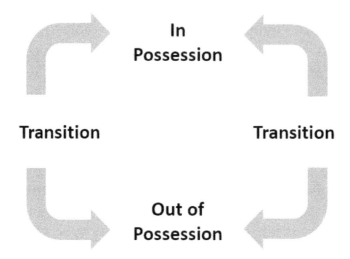

The idea of a game cycle is useful for coaches (and perhaps players) with regards to building a mental model of the game. Within the cycle, exists a possible flaw, though, which is the assumption that the game will always follow the same cycle; that the game is far more ordered and less chaotic than reality sometimes demonstrates.

Here is where we acknowledge that "all models are wrong, but some are useful" (George Box). To help understand the relationship between principles of play, a game cycle is certainly useful, while we should acknowledge the potential for it to be incorrect in a given moment.

Away from these traditional principles of play, there are other concepts to consider, a few of which might be considered universal enough to be principles. The traditional principles brush upon these, without mentioning them specifically.

Create and use space

Werner, Thorpe and Bunker specifically mention space, and a strong case can be made that invasion games are as much about the domination of space as they are about anything (aside from scoring). As with penetration and "go forward", we might consider that the principles of support – width and mobility – are designed to enable the domination of space in-possession, while the out-of-possession principles are designed to control the spaces afforded to the opposition.

Overloads and sub-phases

A way in which teams in-possession can seek an advantage is by creating situations where they outnumber the defenders. The likelihood is that these moments will be momentary and a sub-phase of the game. Depending on the area of the pitch, the probability of whether it is the team in possession, or the team that is out-of-possession, who have a numerical advantage tilts. The tactics of a particular team may also influence this.

For example, a team who do not aim to apply pressure when the opposition have the ball in their own half are allowing the team in-possession an overload in this sub-phase of play. In turn, a team that applies pressure in the opposition half are seeking opportunities to outnumber the team in-possession and force a turnover.

The methods chosen by coaches to achieve the core principles can be considered sub-principles (or even sub-sub-principles). Methods for achieving the core principles fluctuate from team to team and coach to coach. The fluctuations can create fascinating ideologies relating to rotational player movements, counter-pressing, and hundreds of other ideological preferences. All of which may contribute to success but which are – by no means – the only ways to achieve success.

Traditional In-Possession Principles

The traditional principles of play were summarized by Allen Wade while he was director of coaching for the English Football Association. He was keen to point out that he did not create them himself, but collated them and made them easy to understand for the book *The FA Guide to Training and Coaching*. Nonetheless, they have become synonymous with his name and with the emergence of possible alternative principles, and it is quite plausible to describe the traditional principles as the Wade principles. How different the emergent new principles are will be examined later. Although referenced previously, here is the table of principles once again.

The Principles of Play

Attack / In-possession	Defense / Out-of-possession
Penetration	Delay
Support	Depth
Width	Concentration (compaction)
Mobility	Balance
Improvisation/Creativity	Discipline/Patience

Modern interpretations alter the original language from attack and defense into in-possession and out-of-possession. This is in line with the concept of a game cycle (or cycles) and also allows for the possibility that a team's *intention* may define whether they are seeking to attack or defend, and may be more definitive than whether they are in or out-of-possession.

For example, if a team is leading by two goals with ten minutes to go and aims to retain-possession with little to no interest in scoring… are they attacking? At present, our soccer lexicon is insufficient to adequately describe such situations. Defending with the ball would seem to be illogical. Similarly, a team that drops deep out-of-possession in order to draw the opposition forward may be seeking to create space behind the opponents to launch a counter-attack (arguably exercising an attacking principle while not being in possession of the soccer ball!).

Penetration (or "go forward")

The principles of play are often listed in order. Penetration is always number one, while the order in which the other principles appear is variable.

Penetration is the primary aim of invasion games and, without becoming too Freudian, scoring is the ultimate act of penetration. The idea that, at some point, a team needs to go forward in order to score is so fundamental that it is taken for granted, meaning that focus often shifts towards *how* a team decides to go forward. Herein are sub-principles, general principles, or operational principles.

A particular manager or coach may decide that his preference is to play directly into forwards. This forward is then required to be a specific archetype, most likely tall, strong, and powerful in order to act like a wall. Thus, the manager is choosing to bypass the middle area of the pitch in order to penetrate quickly. This can be countered by the opposition, with the defending team limiting how far the attacking team can penetrate by using the offside law, meaning that the forward will not be able to position themselves deep within opposition territory. The territory will not be invaded. This one conceptual battle helps to illustrate the relationships between the principles of play, with the manner in which a principle is executed, thus influencing the manner in which it is countered.

With the use of the offside rule to counter the forward play, the defending team are creating space behind their defense. The archetype of a player previously described may struggle to capitalize on this space, but a different archetype may thrive. The smaller, faster attacker (it should be noted that a player can be tall, strong, powerful, and fast), for example. Thus, the way in which penetration can now occur is not to play directly into the forward, but into the space. In this way, the idea of having a forward pairing with differing attributes became prominent, to prevent a single defensive strategy from nullifying the whole attacking strategy.

A manager or coach may decide that they wish to go forward in a certain way, no matter what personnel are at their disposal. Another manager or coach may decide that the personnel dictate how they go forward. In these two positions, we have the idealist and the pragmatist. At this point, it becomes useful to divide the pitch into thirds in order to understand modern approaches to penetration.

> **"** *It's not about the long ball or the short ball; it's about the right ball.* **"**
>
> **Bob Paisley**

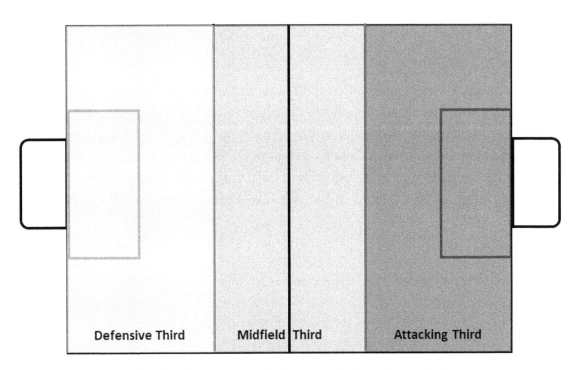

Defensive Third | Midfield | Third | Attacking Third

The direction of attack in the image is from left to right.

For many managers and coaches at the highest levels of soccer, the preference is for a possession-based style. This generally translates into passing the ball through the thirds, building in the defensive third (into the central third), then seeking to create in the final third. This approach requires patience in the final third, and a willingness to begin the process all over again if a good opportunity to penetrate has not been generated. A criticism of this approach is that it can lack penetration as players become unwilling to take risks, favoring retention of the ball over higher risk penetrative passes. These passes are higher risk because the defensive principles dictate that the team out-of-possession will have a greater presence in these areas.

It is here that teams who press and counter-press are more willing to take risks. They are happy to take the risk for, even if the penetrative pass fails, they are presented with an opportunity to counter-press in transition. This is where the game as a cycle can be useful; the moment of transition from in-possession to being wholly out-of-possession is used as an extra chance to mount an attack.

These methods have been preferred by managers such as Guardiola, Bielsa, Klopp and Flick. This does not mean that they are the only methods. In order to go forward, there are many possible methods, but they all spin out from that key principle of penetration.

Example

Chelsea legend Didier Drogba afforded his team tremendous opportunities to go forward. His physical attributes allowed Chelsea to progress up the pitch by playing into his feet, chest, or even head. His strength was such that passes did not have to be perfect to allow Chelsea to move forward into supporting positions once Drogba had retained possession. Not only was Drogba physically strong, but he also possessed enough speed to run onto balls played behind the opposition defense.

Support

The principle of support is often linked to that of movement/mobility. A teammate who is in possession of the ball will generally require passing options. Most simply, these options can be defined as in front, to either side, and behind. In addition to this description, the distance between the teammate and the supporting player should be considered. Therefore, a player requires options with teammates who are within a short pass or (at worst) a medium pass. A further element to consider is whether the supporting options are marked or hiding behind defenders. Passes in straight lines are often easily intercepted or covered, making angled passes more desirable. If we consider the player in-possession to be at the center of a compass with players positioned north, south, east, and west, these options are more easily covered than north-east, north-west, south-east and south-west.

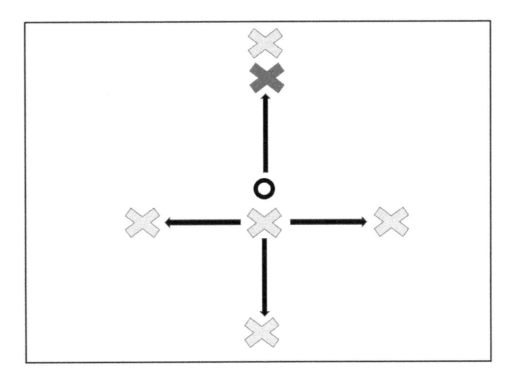

In this image, one passing option is easily blocked.

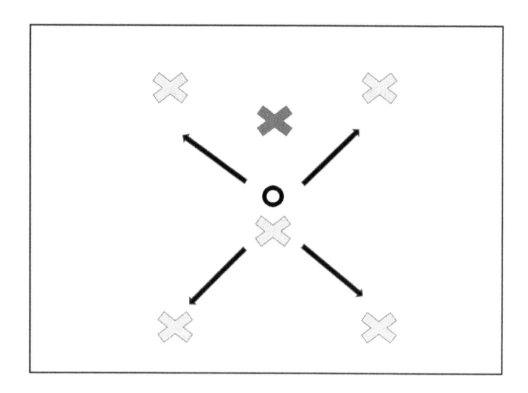

In this image, all passing options remain available.

It is worth noting that players with certain attributes or preferences may need to be supported in different ways. For the player who is an expert dribbler, the best way to support them may involve not going close to them, leaving them enough space to work their magic.

Example

The famed Spain and Barcelona midfield combination of Xavi, Iniesta, and Busquets were masters of possession soccer. While their extraordinary technical abilities undoubtedly played a part in their accomplishments, their ability to offer *appropriate support* to teammates also played a crucial role. As central midfielders, all three players operated predominantly on the interior of the team shape, helping to ensure that the external players always had a passing option while also maintaining their distance between each other. In doing so, the Barcelona team was always within connecting distance, enabling them to dominate possession.

Width

The principle of width is often combined with depth and categorized as *dispersal*. The terminology is in reference to the overall team shape and can be categorized as making the team as long as possible (as great a distance between the central defenders and strikers as possible), and as wide as possible (as great a distance between the wingers or full-backs/wingbacks as possible). The basic idea is that the defensive team will be less able to remain compact centrally and also cover the wide positions. By stretching the team shape, the team in-possession is hoping to create more space for players on the interior as well as the opportunity for overloads in wide areas.

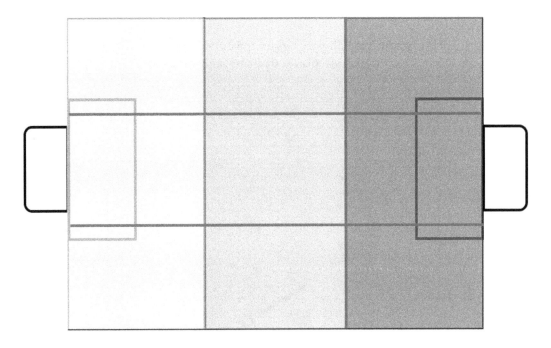

The image shows the pitch divided into thirds – defense, midfield and attack.
These thirds are further divided, with left, center and right sections.
This creates nine possible areas.

By playing quickly to the flanks, teams can avoid congested central areas. From here overlapping or underlapping players (making runs on the outside of players, or on the inside of players) can create numerical superiority in order to create scoring opportunities.

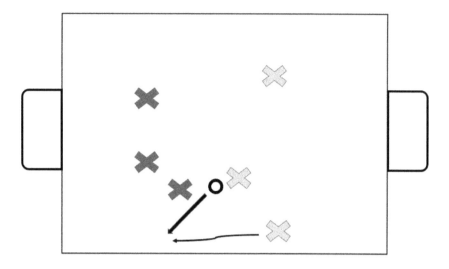

The bottom grey player goes on the outside of the tackling opposition player to create an overlap.

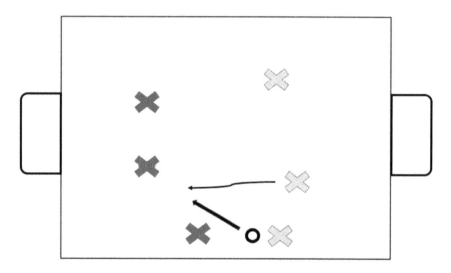

The central grey player moves inside the tackling opposition player to create an underlap.

Should opponents be drawn out to the wide areas, space may be created in central areas or wide on the opposite side of the pitch. The *switch of play* from one side to the other becomes a viable attacking option, either by switching with a single pass, or via two quick passes.

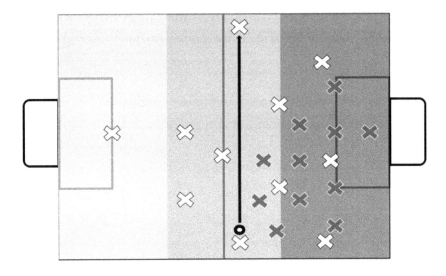

Switch of play in one long pass.

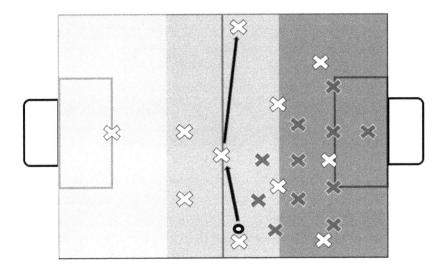

Switch of play in two medium passes.

The use of width is often associated with deliveries from wide areas into the penalty area in order to create chances. Crosses are a viable option for creating scoring opportunities; however, they also come with an element of risk as – in order to increase the chances of scoring from crosses – the attacking team needs to commit players into the penalty area, emptying other areas of the pitch. This could leave them open to the counter-attack.

Some teams have become so wary of this, that they prefer to work the ball into the penalty area to look for cutbacks and low crosses, rather than higher crosses.

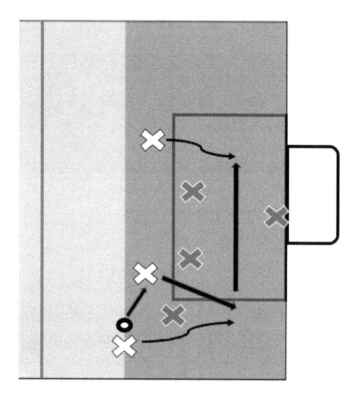

The wide player combines with an internal player, then delivers a low cross.

By spreading the team wide, in-possession, the distances between players can be great. This can leave spaces for counter-attacks. Wary of these, coaches are beginning to play with less width, aiming to play a faster, shorter, passing style *centrally* – in order to decrease the distances between players, enabling them to recover more quickly when they lose possession. This challenges the importance of width as a universal principle.

Example

For many years, a key component of Sir Alex Ferguson's Manchester United sides were what would now be termed orthodox wingers (in the 1990s, they would just have been described as wingers). Ryan Giggs would play as a left-footed winger on the left-hand side with Andrei Kanchelskis as a right-footed winger on the right-hand side. Both players would have starting positions as wide as possible to stretch the pitch vertically. When receiving possession, both players aimed to run or dribble into crossing positions to service the United front two. Similarly, David Beckham looked to occupy wide areas to deliver crosses; however, his position would often be slightly infield to allow Gary Neville the space to overlap.

When Manchester United evolved into a 4-3-3 – with Tevez, Ronaldo, and Rooney as the front three – the Manchester United wide players tucked inside and pushed closer to the central striker, meaning that the team's full-backs were vital for the creation of width with overlapping runs on the outside.

Mobility/Movement

Movement can be sub-categorized in two ways: movement with the ball, and movement without the ball.

Movement with the ball, in essence, describes dribbling or running with the ball. Dribbling can be categorized as tighter, quick, small touches, performed under pressure and often associated with slaloming and twisting movements.

Running with the ball is associated with moving at high speed into spaces with quick, lengthy touches and strides.

Both are forms of penetration – carrying the ball forward and breaking through opposition defenses.

Movement without the ball, or off the ball, can be connected to the principle of support, taking up a certain position in connection to dispersal, or finding space as an individual.

Moving to support a teammate was covered in the support principle. Taking up specific positions may be connected to transition, as a team quickly looks to create an attacking shape after regaining possession. Indeed, should the team be counter-attacking quickly, that movement could be into dangerous attacking positions to enable penetration and the creation of a scoring chance.

If the defending team is set, individual movement is liable to be either to support or find space. Or both. A single player may need to make multiple movements in order to find space depending on their proximity to the defending team's goal.

The closer to the goal they are, the higher the chance that they will be closely marked.

Movement may also manifest in the form of set patterns of movement. An overlap and underlap are examples of this, as are crossover runs, third-man runs, and rotations. All are representative of the differing ways in which this principle may be enacted.

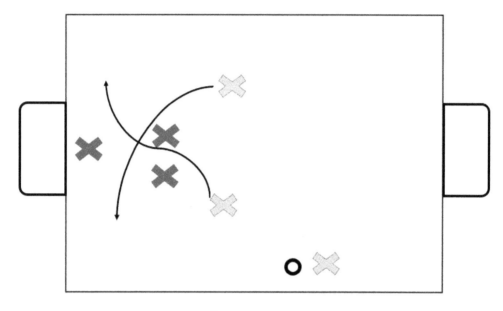

Crossover runs.

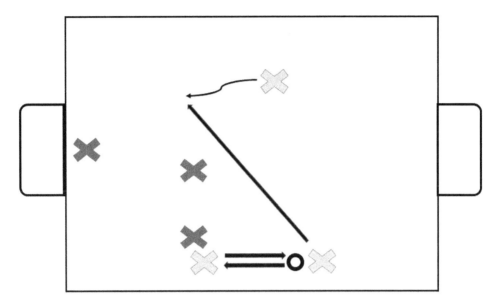

The two wide players combine before passing to the third man.

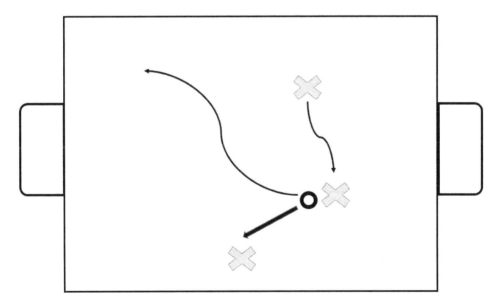

This image illustrates rotation. A player in a deep position makes a forward run after passing. A teammate moves across to cover the vacated space.

Example – Dribble

The history of soccer is littered with incredible dribblers who have left their mark with wonderful goals. Perhaps the two most significant are the diminutive and magical Argentines, Diego Maradona and Lionel Messi. Both have provided numerous examples of solo goals beginning within their own half of the field, and slaloming through opposition defenses before finishing. The most famous of these is Maradona's strike at the 1986 World Cup against England, evading several players at high speed before going around the goalkeeper and slotting into the net. Remarkably, Messi scored an almost identical goal for Barcelona against Getafe as a 19-year-old, announcing his ability to cause havoc against opposition teams with his ability to progress the ball forward through the art of dribbling.

Example – Off the ball

Movement off the ball can also be effective. The English midfielders of David Platt and Frank Lampard were skilled at moving away from the ball and arriving in opposition penalty areas. From these positions, they finished off numerous attacking moves. These runs were sometimes just a case of good timing to arrive in space. On other occasions, multiple movements were executed with initial movements designed to deceive defenders before moving into areas they actually wanted to receive the ball. Recently, Erling Haaland has developed a signature movement in which his first movement is towards the far post before darting in front of the defender – to the near post – and finishing.

Improvisation/Creativity

Creativity in all aspects of life is extraordinarily hard to define. What might be creative to one person might be run of the mill to another. Academic definitions do not make it much easier, either. The terminology used is one of "tactical creativity" – the ability to produce work that is both novel and appropriate, surprising, original, and flexible. Precisely what 'this is' is elusive, but what's certain is that we recognize it when we see it, even if we struggle to describe it.

What is sure is that the more successful teams tend to be more creative. Teams that are successful generally score more goals than their competitors, and to do so they will penetrate more often, creating opportunities. The better the team becomes, or the greater their reputation, the more cautious teams will be against them, with space becoming harder to find. Going forward will be a difficult task, and the principle of improvisation and creativity will become more important.

We can therefore view improvisation and creativity as desirable principles or attributes to possess, although that does not mean that it is impossible to win games of soccer without them.

Example

With defenses becoming increasingly packed, and space becoming more and more limited, the ability to provide moments of imagination and creativity is increasingly important. Certain players provide these moments with more regularity than others. Dribbling is often a source of improvisation and creativity, but a pass or finish can also provide inspiration. Dennis Bergkamp, Cesc Fabregas, and Mesut Ozil possessed the ability to find a pass, improvising with different techniques such as scooping the ball over defenses, stabbing with the toes, or spinning the ball with the inside or outside of the pass.

Other players improvise unorthodox finishes. Ronaldinho offers a famous example, against Chelsea, when he punted a strike with his toes from outside the penalty area while under pressure from Chelsea defenders. The technique enabled him to get the shot away quickly and deceived the goalkeeper. In turn, his Brazilian compatriot, Romario, excelled at quick, poked finishes with the toes. A technique that he performed so regularly that it became commonplace for him, but remained unusual for others.

My game is based on improvisation.
Often a forward does not have the time
to think too much. You have a second,
rarely more, to decide whether to dribble,
shoot or pass to the right or left.

Ronaldinho

Traditional Out-of-Possession Principles

Delay

The antonym of penetration and go forward. The primary objective of a team or individual that is out-of-possession is to prevent their opponents from creating or scoring, which makes preventing them from playing forward quickly desirable. The concept is fundamentally basic, but there are varying and contrary methods to carry out the principle.

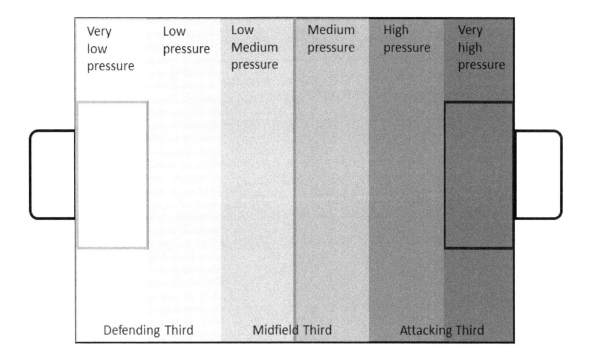

Coaches may decide on a method of delay that suits their personnel, their ideology, or which is based on what they know of the opposition's strengths and weaknesses.

A team who press/counter-press will place an emphasis on delaying the opponent close to their own goal – through the pressure of individuals or the attacking unit. How this pressure is applied may be trigger-dependent and/or transition-dependent. If the team have just turned over possession, they will attempt to regain-possession as quickly as possible. The pressure that they apply could be enough to delay the attack; however, in applying pressure, the opportunity to bypass a unit of the team might be presented. Thus, there is a need to create *defensive layers*, wherever the pressure is being applied. These layers could be characterized as an element of the principle of depth.

A pressing team may also delay the opposition by pressuring passing lines rather than directly pressuring players. In this way, a smaller number of out-of-possession players can delay a larger number of in-possession players.

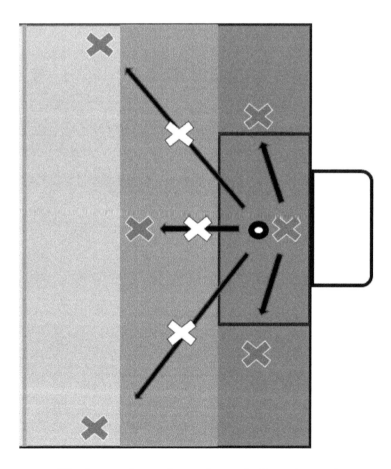

The image shows three players influencing and reducing the number of passing options available.

In the previous image, three forwards (in white) impede the ability of the goalkeeper and defensive unit to build with short passes through their positioning. The central player prevents a simple straight pass. The two side players are close enough to threaten short passes (if they are played), and also prevent easy passes to the players in the light grey areas.

Conversely, a team may decide to delay the opposition by not applying pressure high, but by dropping back and placing bodies between the opposition and the goal. A roadblock to deny space and a clear path forward.

In a more fundamental way, the principle of delay can be seen as simply blocking the path to goal. This can manifest as a defender positioning their body between the ball and the goal, blocking a pass or shot, or removing the ball from a dangerous position. The goalkeeper making a save might even be considered a delaying action as it has delayed the ball from entering the goal!

As with penetration, delay is usually listed first when it comes to out-of-possession and defensive principles. The remaining principles contribute to how the out-of-possession team delay the opponent.

Example

A key part of Liverpool's strategy during Jurgen Klopp's time as manager has been in preventing the opposition from using short passing on goal kicks in order to progress the ball down the field. Liverpool spend many hours on the training pitch working on the signature front three of Salah, Mane, and Firmino in *three versus six scenarios* – covering passing lines and applying pressure at the appropriate moment. While understanding angles, distances, and positioning are vital, so too is practicing together to be in tune with each other's actions.

*The formula to beat the press is simple;
it's the execution that's tough. If you
have the quality to do so, you pass your
way through it. If you don't, you just
boot it over the top. Then it becomes a
game of winning 'second balls'.*

Carlo Ancelotti

Depth

The defensive principle of depth has multiple applications. Depth supports the principle of delay and – in some documents – the principle is referred to as *defensive support*. A key idea that has featured in coach education is with 2v2 situations, with the closest player to the ball engaging and applying pressure. The second defender is in a position where they are close enough to the attacker without the ball, but also close enough to help their defensive partner. The defender who is supporting is *not* level with their teammate's shoulder but slightly staggered, behind, and at an angle – creating depth. This "job and a half" sub-phase illustrates the support of teammates by providing depth and cover.

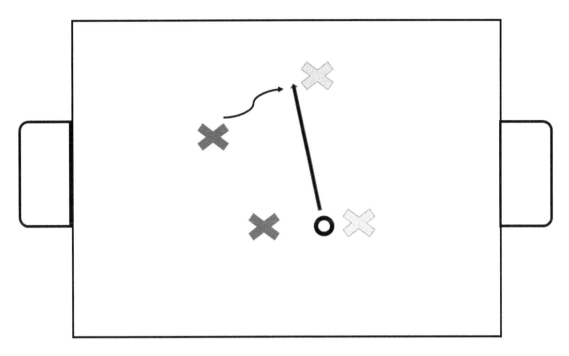

This image illustrates defensive positioning and pressure when working as a pair.

More often than not, out-of-possession depth relates to the positioning of the deepest defensive line in relation to halfway and the edge of the defending team's penalty area. The choice of where this line is positioned is related to strategy. This strategy could be ideological or pragmatic, rooted in preferential ideas of how soccer teams best defend, or based on knowledge of the strengths of the team and the opposition.

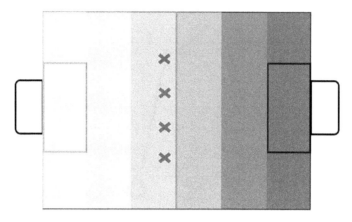

High defensive line.

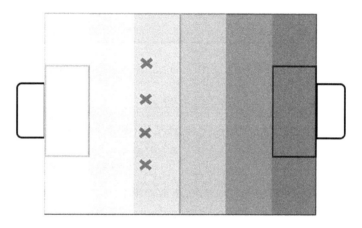

Medium/Deep defensive line.

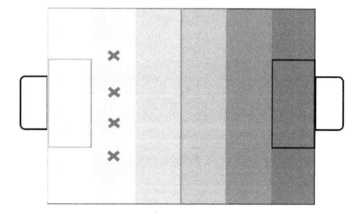

Deep defensive line.

Depth may also be applied to the concept of creating defensive lines or layers. Each unit of the team looks to come together to create a barrier, forcing the team in-possession to penetrate each line or layer systematically to create a good scoring opportunity. The layers can be attack, midfield, defense, and goalkeeper, but it is also possible to redistribute the positioning of the midfield to generate further layering. Creation of these layers requires a team to be well-organized and have a shared understanding of their objective.

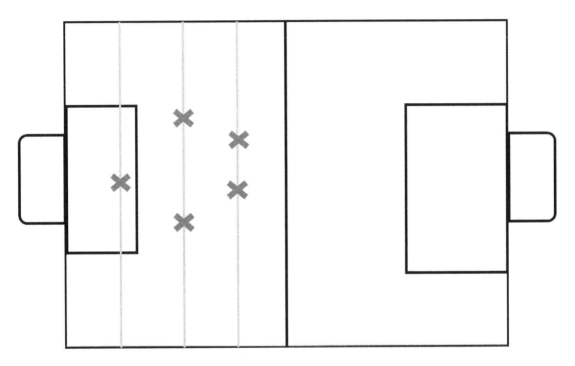

Principles do not only apply to 11v11 soccer. Here layers are created in a 5v5. A "box" (2 and 2) creates two layers with the goalkeeper forming a third layer.

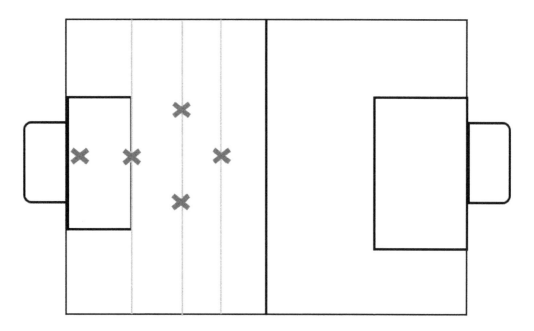

Here a 5v5 uses a "diamond" shape (1-2-1) creating three layers with the goalkeeper forming a fourth layer.

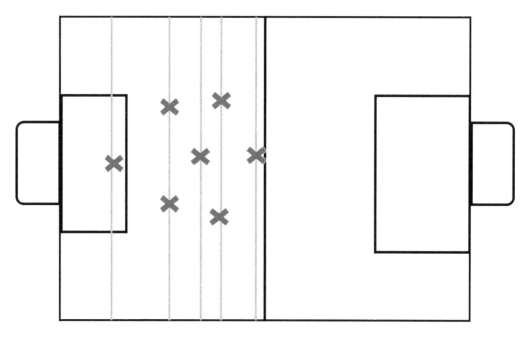

Here layers are created in 7v7 soccer. The six outfield players form four layers with the goalkeeper creating a fifth layer.

Example

Leicester City's 2015/16 Premier League title-winning team was founded (famously) on a deep defensive line in order to draw the opposition high up the pitch, creating spaces to counter-attack into once a turnover occurred. Leicester kept their defenders back – inside their own half – even when their in-possession position was deep in opposition territory.

In contrast, Bayern Munich conquered Europe in 2020 with an extremely high defensive line. When their in-possession position was high in the opposition half, Manuel Neuer (their goalkeeper) would often be the only player inside their own half. Indeed, his positioning would be well outside of the penalty area in the "sweeper-keeper" role.

Concentration (Compaction)

The term concentration *does not* relate to focus, and can be quite confusing. This is probably why it is typically followed by the word compaction.

To comprehend concentration and compaction, we must consider the concept of *dispersal* when in-possession.

In our example, the team in-possession has sought to spread themselves out, making the playing area "big". This will mean that certain positions or points will have large distances between them. When a team loses the ball, and move out-of-possession, they aim to group closer together to close the gaps (as part of the transition principles). The tightly-grouped defensive unit is described as compact. More often than not, this group would be centrally positioned in line with the goals and the space immediately to the side of the goals (width of the penalty area or even more narrow).

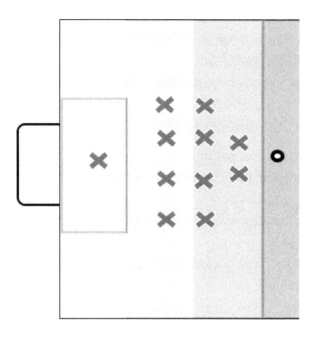

A compact team creating a dense block between the ball and the goal.

A compact team seeks to deny the in-possession team any space that they can exploit with forward passes or dribbles. They are, quite simply, blocking a direct path to goal. At a minimum, the compaction aims to only allow spaces that the in-possession team will find more difficult to exploit, either because this space is less threatening on the goal, or because the in-possession team lacks the attributes to effectively exploit this space.

Example

Under Diego Simeone, Atletico Madrid have consistently lined up in a 4-4-2 formation. The team defend very narrowly, with little space between teammates. The right- and left-sided midfielders tuck in alongside the central midfielders while one or both strikers also drop deep as an additional screen in front of the midfield (or they mark the opposition holding midfielder). The whole team shifts with the movement of the ball (like a shoal of fish) to maintain the barricade, waiting for the right moment to step out of the shape to challenge for possession, but preferring to wait for an interception.

.

Balance

The out-of-possession team will seek to maintain an appropriate numerical distribution when defending. Remembering that the primary principle is *delay* (which prevents the opposition from scoring), the out-of-possession team should prioritize defending the goal. It would be logical to position players as close to the goal as possible. However, it is also prudent to defend the ball. Therefore, the out-of-possession team will position themselves in relation to the position of the ball in relation to the goal. While the team who are defending must be wary of (and aware of) opposition players, they can afford to leave players who are far from both the ball and the goal free as they pose little threat. In doing so, the defending team will be balanced.

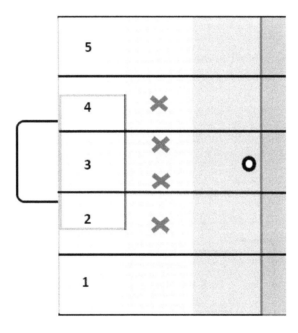

With the ball positioned centrally, the four defenders cover the central areas. Wide areas are left free.

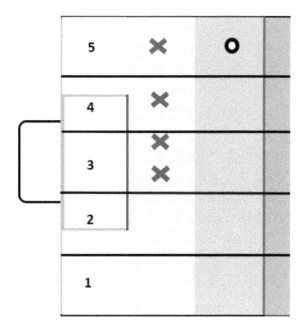

As the ball has moved to the right of the pitch (defense's left) the defense has shifted across, leaving the two zones furthest from the ball free.

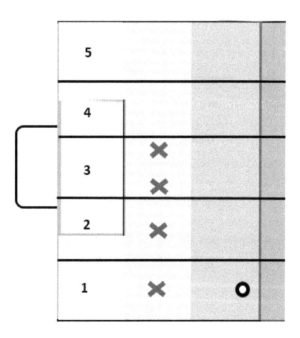

As the ball has moved to the left of the pitch (defense's right) the defense has shifted across, leaving the two zones furthest from the ball free.

For out-of-possession teams, it is most difficult to achieve balance during transition and counter-attacks. These situations are often described as being "out of balance" due to players being out of position or the attacking team having gained numerical superiority. Out-of-possession teams will seek to outnumber in-possession teams. It is very rare for the team out-of-possession to be satisfied with mere numerical equality. The out-of-possession team will seek numerical superiority whenever possible; thus, in stable periods of play, balance is not equal but actually tilted *towards the out-of-possession side*.

Example

Maintaining a balanced defensive unit has been critical to the success of many teams. The balance can be impacted, however, by not sliding across effectively – as the ball is moved – to maintain the right distances between the defenders. This rarely happens at the elite levels of soccer. What is far more likely to impact the balance of the backline is the manner in which a team pushes forward their full-backs when in-possession. During Mourinho's first period at Chelsea they often only pushed the full-back forward on the side of the pitch where the ball was located, leaving the opposite full-back to remain alongside the central defenders. Tony Pulis went further with Stoke City, often playing with full-backs who were comfortable playing as central defenders and keeping both back, alongside the central defenders, to ensure that the balance and distances between players would be extremely hard to break. Pulis was happy to sacrifice attacking opportunities for greater guarantees of defensive security.

Discipline/Patience

A player's location on the pitch influences patience, as does the team strategy.

Defenders will need to be judicious in their decision-making as to whether they should attempt to regain the ball. Making an impatient choice can open defensive gaps, making the job of the opponent easier than it might have been had the defender chosen to just stand their ground, (e.g., choosing to delay rather than risking a regain). Should there be suitable support, then the risk to regain is lower due to a teammate being able to provide cover.

The amount of pressure that an out-of-possession team seeks to apply will affect how disciplined/patient they need to be. If the strategy is to apply immediate pressure high up the pitch, less discipline or patience is required. If the strategy is to block passing lines, then more discipline will be required.

Midfielders may be required to hold their position rather than seek out the ball, occupying spaces that (if left unattended) may seriously impede the out-of-possession team's ability to defend. This is not dissimilar to defensive players remaining in close proximity to the goal they are defending. The priority becomes to stand ground and block the offensive path. Regaining the ball is a lower priority when compared to the risk of conceding a goal.

Example

The performance of Inter Milan against Barcelona in 2010 is the archetype for stopping a high-quality attacking side that is capable of blitzing even the most capable of opponents. This game also saw Jose Mourinho and Pep Guardiola match up against each other.

A Barcelona side replete with Messi, Ibrahimovic, Xavi, Busquets and many others were kept at bay by the tactics of Jose Mourinho. Mourinho plugged the middle of the pitch, denying Barcelona's players the space in which they preferred to operate. In doing so, they sacrificed the wide areas, allowing Barcelona to cross if they chose to, backing Inter's defensive duo of Lucio and Walter Samuel to win the aerial duels. Inter's defensive plan was intelligent and required discipline, but it also required intense focus, concentration, and desire.

Transition

Compared to the other principles of play, the term transition is a relatively new addition. It is most often used to describe the moment (or moments) when a turnover in possession occurs.

Transition is not a passage of play that teams will *seek* to create, but it is a passage that teams will seek to exploit or control. It can be seen as a moment to win or lose, and many coaches believe that if you win the transitions, you will win the game.

Transition has been sub-categorized into positive and negative phases within the game cycle. Whether the turnover is characterized as positive or negative will depend on whether a team has just regained or lost possession.

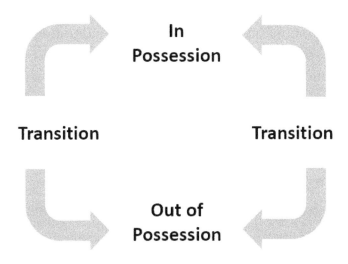

Positive Transition

The objective of positive transition (or regaining possession) will generally be to attack as quickly as possible. This is connected to the in-possession principle of penetration/go forward. Teams who have turned over possession will be lacking in defensive balance and have left spaces to be exploited.

When this situation has been established, in-possession principles come into play.

In essence, a race is formed between the team who experienced positive transition and the team who experienced negative transition to get organized and appropriately positioned (with in-possession and out-of-possession principles being applied at amplified speed).

Can the counter-attacking team create an opportunity to score before the recovering defensive team can get into a position with suitable depth, cover, and balance? When the out-of-possession team has recovered and achieved balance, the counter-attack is over, and the game resumes at normal speed.

Teams are coached into how positive transitions should unfold. The most common of these apply to the *speed of the attack, where* the transition has occurred, and the *player* who has regained possession.

As the counter-attack is reliant on rapid attacking, time limits or a specific numbers of passes can be applied to guide the action. At one time, England youth teams used a 6-6-6 rule.

- Can the team attack with at least six players?
- Can the team progress into the opposition half in six passes or fewer?
- Can the team regain-possession within six seconds of losing it?

The first two rules encouraged fast attacking and for players to get forward in support of the players in attack. Unsurprisingly, a player who attempts to counter-attack alone is unlikely to be successful.

As a strategy, teams will focus their regaining of possession in specific areas. Any such strategy will also relate to negative transition, but the objective of negative transition may be to create a positive transition as quickly as possible. Should a team aim to regain the ball close to the opposition goal, different support will be required, and different passes will be required (in comparison to regaining possession close to a team's own goal). The spaces available to exploit will also differ.

The status of a player regaining the ball will also impact the possibilities of counter-attacking. If a player has just made a tackle to regain the ball, *that player* is possibly poorly positioned to attack themselves. The player is also likely to have been focused on the ball and have a poor awareness of the situation on the pitch. Many coaches encourage this player to quickly play a short pass to a teammate.

Example

A decade ago, the Manchester United forward line of Rooney, Ronaldo, and Tevez punished the opposition with counter-attacks. Ronaldo possessed exceptional pace, and whilst Rooney or Tevez were not especially rapid sprinters, both could move quickly enough, more important to their success was their speed of thought and recognition of space.

The team most famously destroyed Arsenal in the Champions League in 2008/9, and one play from that match stands out where, holding a comfortable lead, a sweeping move sealed the victory.

In the 60th minute, Arsenal delivered a corner from their right-hand side. A defensive header cleared the ball to Ronaldo approximately 10 meters outside the United penalty area. From Ronaldo's lay off, a pass was punched out by Park Ji-sung to United's left side, and Rooney took the ball and ran at the defense. Moments later, he fizzed a low pass across the Arsenal box to Ronaldo who fired home. The move was over in four passes and five seconds!

❝ *It is my job to help the players react better.* **❞**

Jurgen Klopp

Negative transition

Should a team turnover possession, they experience negative transition. Whilst the terminology of positive and negative are the (currently) favored descriptions, they quite literally carry positive and negative connotations that may not be accurate.

Fundamentally, any team that loses possession will seek to regain possession at some point. If their priority is to regain possession as quickly as possible, they will pressure aggressively. If their priority is *not to concede*, they will prioritize organizing themselves into a balanced structure. The 6-6-6 rule referenced above suggests that players attempt to regain the ball for six seconds after losing possession. Barcelona under Guardiola had a similar rule, and many teams have used variations on a five- or six-second rule. When that time is up, players no longer pressure to regain the ball – they drop into organized defensive positions.

The idea of counter-pressing has gained popularity and become particularly associated with German soccer. A counter-pressing team aims to win the negative transition, using it as an opportunity to launch a counter-attack.

Countering the counter is potentially even more devastating as a team transitions from being out-of-possession, into being in possession, and will then have to transition once again to being out-of-possession, all in an incredibly short time frame. The defensive structure and balance will be weaker and exploitable.

Example

Pep Guardiola's Barcelona side employed a five-second rule to regain possession after a turnover. Training sessions were developed specifically to improve the players' reactions to losing possession. At RB Leipzig, meanwhile, Ralf Ragnick used a metronome, ticking down the seconds within which players had to regain-possession.

Calculated pressing became popular after AC Milan's success in the late 1980s and early 1990s under Arrigo Saachi, though it is arguable that English clubs Wimbledon and Watford used a form of counter-pressing, turning the opposition with long balls into space and fighting for loose balls. The globalization of soccer, with coaches moving freely from nation to nation, has seen pressing and counter-pressing become commonplace.

We like to press high, with a very intense counter-pressure. When we have the ball, we do not like square or back passes.

Ralf Rangnick

So, here ends the first part of the book. For some of you, this may be enough – a rundown into the principles of play.

The next section looks at alternative principles, so please join us as we dig deeper into soccer's foundations.

Alternative Principles

Each national governing body is responsible for its own coach education. While all UEFA licenses would appear to carry the same weight, they are far from identical. A certain number of elements must be included in order to be ratified by UEFA, but the precise content, number of hours required, and depth of information are variable.

Some principles (as per this book's first section) use different language but are highly similar to traditional principles. Other principles are alluded to in the traditional principles or not mentioned at all.

It should also be noted that some national governing bodies have more principles than others, also using the term 'concepts' rather than principles. Whether these are universal principles, or not, they are likely to be useful for coaches to be aware of.

Possession/Own the ball/Want to have and keep possession of the ball

For some nations, possession in itself is a principle. The retention of the ball and staying in-possession is highly prized. The purpose of this possession may not be to "go forward" for some nations state that vertical passes are not a preference. The premise is that the team who owns the ball will win the majority of their games; however, it is very difficult to win without going forward at some point! Exactly how and where teams retain possession is left open to interpretation.

In-possession, eleven men have to be in motion. Busy fine-tuning distances. It's not a question of how much you run but where you run to.

Johan Cruyff

Defend By Retaining Possession of the Ball

Without the need to "go forward", possession becomes a means to prevent the opposition from scoring. It is extremely unusual for a team to score without having some form of possession of the ball (in 2017, Estonian side Paide conceded an own goal after just 14 seconds; the opponents, Levadia, had not touched the ball). Possession can become negative, or stagnant, without the intent to attack the opponent's goal. Certain game situations might demand this, of course, but the preferences of individual coaches may mean that the same situation has multiple solutions. A possession-hungry coach may decide that when being ahead 1-0 with five minutes remaining, the best way to win the game would be to retain the ball for those five minutes, winding the clock down and starving the opponent of the ball. Other coaches might decide that territory is more important than possession and have their players clear the ball as far into the opposition half as possible.

The influence of Pep Guardiola, as a coach, seeped through Spanish soccer. In 2008, Spain were crowned European Champions, and their playing style melded elements of what had become known as tiki-taka and a faster-paced, more traditional Spanish style.

In 2010, Spain became World Champions, with their style of play wholly reflecting that of Barcelona at their best – highly dominant in-possession, while still possessing a thrust going forward.

By 2012, the style had prioritized possession. Opposition teams now dropped extremely deep, giving Spain what they wanted, waiting for an error in-possession. Spain won the 2012 Euros, but games were very low scoring and Spain conceded very few goals. Their possession had become a defensive tool, simply starving the opposition of the ball and denying them attacking opportunities.

Strong Position Play

Positional play is most strongly associated with Spanish soccer and the phrase "Juego de posicion". Positional play divides the pitch into zones, with each player being assigned a zone or zones.

Each zone carries different expectations of the player. Players are not necessarily fixed within a zone, but should they leave a zone it is expected that another player rotates into their space. The traditional principles of mobility, support, and width come into play as concepts that enable effective positional play.

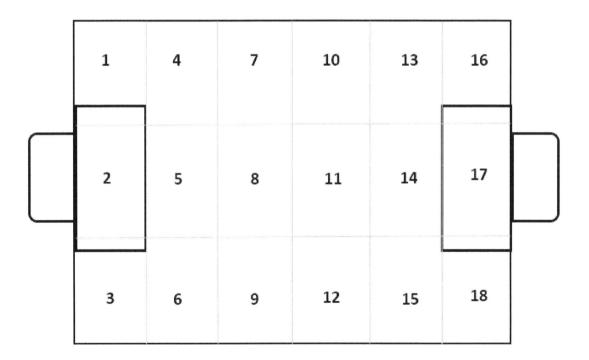

Illustration of zones on a soccer pitch, including the once vital zone 14.

Example

The division of the pitch into zones is key for Juego de posicion. The zones on the pitch are not only related to the roles that fill them, or the actions expected, but also operate as triggers. Should they all be in a certain zone, that tells players that other zones need to be occupied. If the ball is in the right midfield area, the positions to be occupied are different to those when the ball is in the left-hand half-space. The whole team is required to make shifts as the ball moves. Sir Alex Ferguson described playing against Guardiola's Barcelona as like being on a carousel, reflecting on their constant movement.

Finding Space to Receive the Ball

Movement and mobility are traditional principles whose outcomes include individuals finding space. It should be noted that it is quite possible for players to find space without moving; if others move from one area into another, space is made available. Indeed, the awareness of players to identify space might be more important than their ability to move at speed.

Playing in the Spaces

Playing in the spaces is another principle that is deeply interconnected to other principles. The principles flow from one into the other.

Strong positional play suggests that each zone has its own set of priorities. Therefore, the finding of space alone is not enough; rather, understanding what each area *embodies* is vital. At one point in time, zone 14 was considered to be the hub of chance creation on the soccer pitch, which meant that teams would work extremely hard to control that area and get technically superior players in-possession in zone 14.

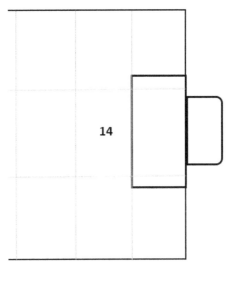

Zone 14.

In response to this out-of-possession scenario, teams would utilize a player whose job was to occupy zone 14, denying creative players space. In response, the team in-possession sought to utilize the very edges of zone 14, seeking to get creative players on the verges of zone 13 and 14 and the verges of zone 15 and 14. These areas became elongated and known as the half-spaces.

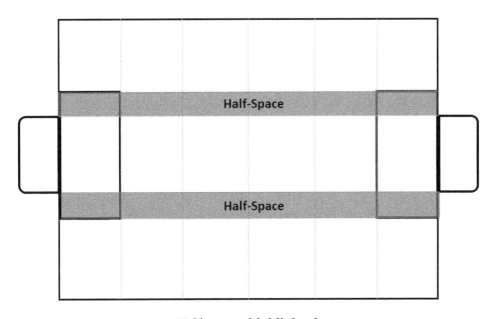

Half-spaces highlighted.

Teams then began to mark out their training pitches to reflect the zones they sought to position themselves in. Coaches will use different grids to reflect their positional objectives.

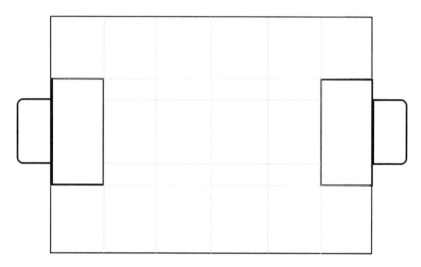

Pitch divided to highlight the attacking, midfield, and defensive thirds. Pitch further divided to show wide areas and half-spaces. This setup is famously used by Pep Guardiola.

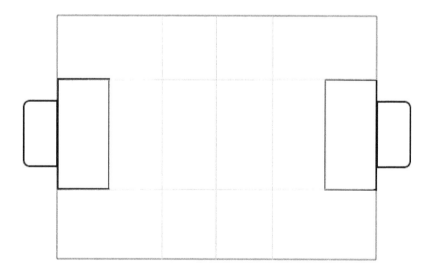

Pitch divided to represent the attacking, midfield and defensive thirds. Each third is further divided into left, center, and right. In the midfield third, the area is split further to represent attacking and defensive midfield roles. The above has been used by former Chelsea and Tottenham Hotspur manager Andre Villas-Boas, and other club coaches.

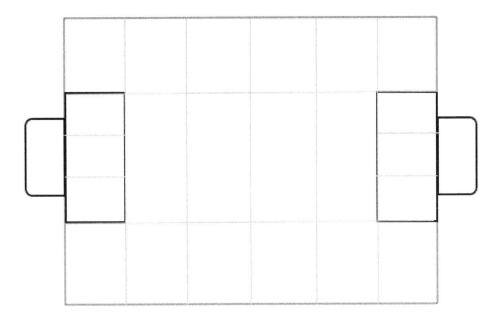

Pitch divided to aid building up from goal kicks with additional zones within the penalty area and in the fullback/wing positions.

Example

Kevin De Bruyne has a well-earned reputation as one of the most prolific providers of assists in world soccer. A high proportion of those assists come from the left- and right-half-spaces. The left-hand half-space sees De Bruyne slip low, relatively short passes through the defense. In the right-hand half-space, De Bruyne creates with what has become a trademark curved pass to the far post.

 It's not a case that one player is in a particular lane, it doesn't matter who it is, but it is important that we occupy the pitch.

Dan Micciche

Using the Width and Depth of the Pitch

Width is included amongst the traditional in-possession principles. However, it is difficult to discuss width without depth and dispersal. Connecting the principles of width and depth, positional play, movement (finding space), and playing in spaces, creates a guide to forming a team shape when in possession. Certain team shapes and formations may, at first, appear to lack width until the off-the-ball movement of players is understood.

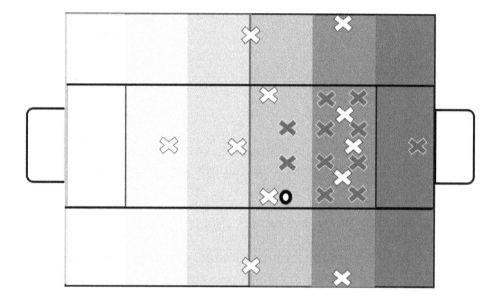

Team shape with deep and high width on both sides of the pitch.
The three forwards provide high options centrally.

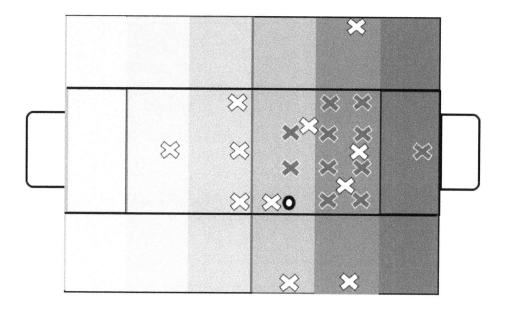

Team shape with deep and high width on the side of the pitch where the ball is.
In this shape, there is only high width on the side of the pitch opposite to the ball.
The two forwards are offset and one provides a high option.

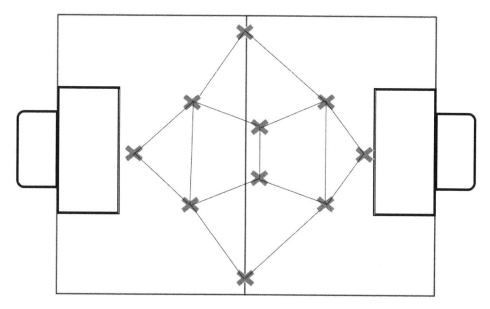

The positions are linked together in a web of passing lines.

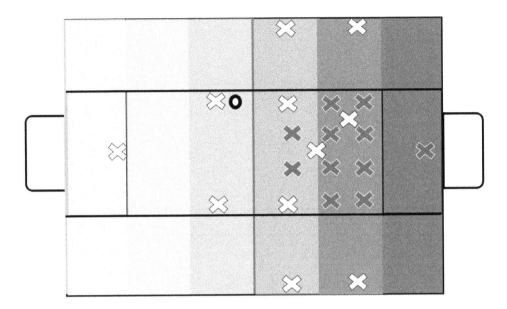

In this shape, the central defenders are positioned deeper (as is the goalkeeper). Both full-backs have pushed wide along with the wingers. There are two wide options on both sides of the pitch. This shape has only one striker providing a high option centrally.

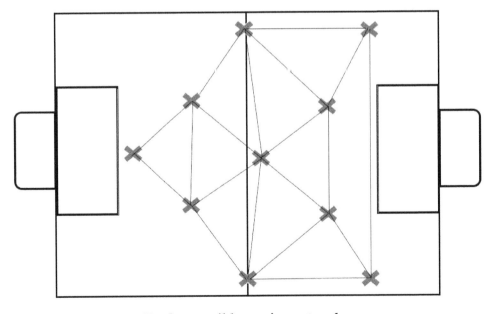

Further possible passing networks.

Play in The Opponent's Half as Much as Possible

Playing in the opponent's half, as much as possible, is a logical step towards victory as the team will have possession closer to the opposition goal. Similarly, the ball will be further from the attacking team's goal, in theory meaning it would take the opposition longer to score should a turnover occur. This concept may also impact the positioning of the team in-possession, squeezing into the opposition half, which may be beneficial in connection to a pressing strategy. This principle may also indicate the prioritization of territory over possession.

Play Forward Early and Consolidate Possession

Again, prizing territory, a team (or coach) looks to move the ball into opposition territory to establish a foothold, before consolidating possession. By playing forward early, a team will have the opportunity to counter-attack should there be enough space to do so, thus blending in-possession and transition principles. When there is no counter-attack opportunity, a team will seek to retain possession.

Example

RB Leipzig have developed a fast, intense soccer style. Progressing the ball slowly and methodically from defensive areas is not a priority; their preference is to look to play into the final third as early as possible to establish a foothold from which to build possession. As well as having a metronome to dictate pressing, the coach brought in a subsequent ten-second metronome as a shot clock during practice. The team in-possession has to aim for a shot at goal within ten seconds from the moment possession begins.

Fast Counter-Attacking

Some governing bodies actively prioritize counter-attacking over possession. Both are a means to penetrate, although fast counter-attacking is more reliant upon transitional concepts than in-possession concepts. Both methods can be successful, which would suggest that neither has a particular edge, but will exist within a given moment.

High Pressure When the Ball is Lost (5-Second Rule)

A transition principle designed to launch counter-attacks close to the opposition goal. Strongly associated with German and Spanish soccer styles before being adopted elsewhere.

 While the opponent has the ball, the whole team presses, always trying to cut off the play as close as possible to the opponent's goal; when we get it, we look to play with dynamism and create the spaces for improvisation.

Marcelo Bielsa

Winning the Ball Back Quickly in High and Middle Areas With an Aggressive Pressing Game (5-6 Seconds of Aggressive Pressing, Especially When The Ball is Lost in Middle Areas)

This is a highly-specific counter-pressing style with the intention to regain possession centrally. This method of pressing is explicitly designed to take advantage of teams who have regained position and who are transitioning their team shape from compact (concentrated) into dispersed (wide and deep). When transitioning, gaps will be created which may be exploited.

Show Opponents Outside as Much as You Can

An individual, unit or entire team orientates itself to prevent the opposition penetrating the central areas of the pitch. In doing so, they are prepared to allow the opposition territory and possession in wide areas. This can also be referred to as *making play predictable*. Taken to an extreme degree, it can involve not just deflecting the play into wide areas, but actively conceding space as those spaces are not considered to carry as much of a threat.

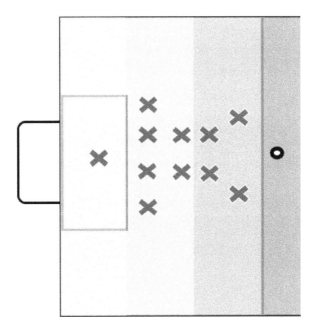

Example

The performance of Jose Mourinho's Inter Milan team against Barcelona in 2010 remains the prime example of an extreme version of showing the opposition the flanks of the pitch, but there have been many other deployments of the strategy. A newly-promoted Norwich City side visited Liverpool in 2011 and visibly allowed Liverpool to dominate wide areas and rain crosses into their area, backing themselves to win the headers. Those headed clearances became opportunities to counter-attack as Liverpool's midfield committed to the Norwich penalty area. Norwich secured a valuable 1-1 draw. Similar tactics would be used against Manchester United in the post-Ferguson era, leading to an infamous game at home to Fulham where they pumped 81 crosses in during a single game. The game was drawn.

 This is what a good manager does — you study and think and discuss, and you come up with a model of playing.

Carlo Ancelotti

By combining these principles, a governing body or organization can create their own game or cycle. These models often say more about the ideology and identity of the entity.

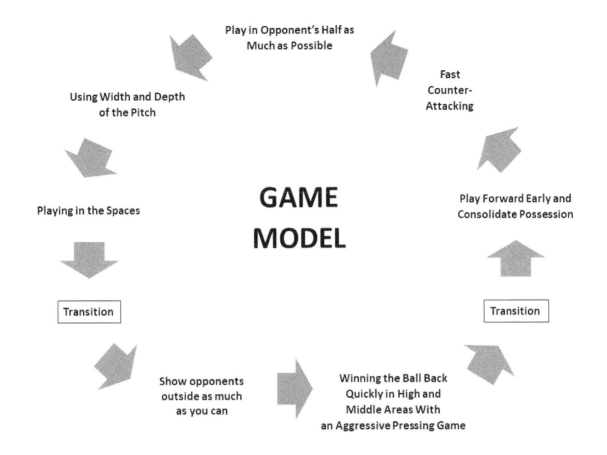

The above model combines the elements needed to create a plausible game model. The repeated theme remains playing forward when in-possession, and preventing the opposition from playing forward when out-of-possession. All other principles and concepts relate to how these actions might occur. For instance, a team does not have to play forward early; they might choose to play forward relatively late to secure possession. A team may decide to show the opponents inside rather than outside if the area is packed with supporting defenders. Playing in spaces could be a more universal principle, but some players require very little space in order to succeed.

Academic Principles

Further to the traditional principles of Allen Wade, and the Football Association and the principles of national governing bodies, academics have developed principles for soccer.

Renowned academic figures Daniel Bouthier, Jean-Francis Gréhaigne, Paul Godbout, Filipe Manuel Clemente, and others, have dedicated time to identifying principles that guide strategy and tactics in soccer and other invasion games.

Their research suggests that team sports are directed by different kinds of principles, namely: general principles, operational principles, and fundamental principles. The traditional principles that we have covered previously in the book fit within these categories, forming the fundamental principles, with additional principles expanding the concepts.

Deception Principle

It has been suggested that a fundamental concept of invasion games is to outwit the opposition. There's no formula as to how such actions are carried out but by making our opponent believe that we are carrying one action or plan – and then executing another – we can encourage them to make mistakes which can then be exploited.

For an individual in-possession, this deception principle can be applied to dribbling and the use of dribbling moves (often described as skills but possibly better described as tricks) to put out-of-possession opponents off-balance and out of position. For a player who is seeking to receive the ball, and finding space, the deception principle takes the form of double movements – the first to make the defender believe they are seeking a specific space, before quickly moving into the space they actually wish to occupy.

Example

Of the many ways to deceive an opponent, Riyad Mahrez has mastered the fake shot. His movements convince defenders that a strike or pass is coming, manipulating them into a blocking position in order to go past them. Another method used to deceive defenders is to leave the ball, letting it run through the legs and on to a teammate. Dwight Yorke and Andy Cole famously combined for a goal against Barcelona that began with a pass into Dwight Yorke who stepped over the ball, allowing it to go through to Andy Cole. The two players then played a one-two through the Barcelona defense allowing Cole to score.

Surprise Principle

Unsurprisingly, the surprise principle is intricately linked to the deception principle and traditional principles of creativity and imagination.

When in-possession, a team or individual is more likely to unbalance those out-of-possession if those out-of-possession players cannot predict what is coming next. Surprise may come from a coach applying the principles of play in an unexpected way (this does not have to be something novel, merely not what the opponent would expect) or from an individual producing an original action. An action that is flexible, fluent, unusual, and original. These are the moments that delight observers and are capable of not only changing matches but the perceptions of the sport itself.

Example

In 1974, Johan Cruyff shocked the world with his turn at the World Cup. The move is now commonplace at training grounds around the globe, but at the time no one had ever seen it before. The move took everyone by surprise.

Likewise, when teams first fielded a line up without a designated center-forward, oppositions were caught by surprise. More recently, Sheffield United's use of overlapping central defenders has caught opponents by surprise.

One of the beauties of soccer is that the game affords opportunities to surprise.

Mobility Principle

Mobility/movement appear to be fundamental to gameplay. Movement refers to both the movement of individuals and the movement of the ball. Fast-shifting ball circulation is considered of vital importance for enabling the invasion of opposition territory. The ball is being circulated in an effort to move the out-of-possession team away from the center of the pitch; drawing them away from the target area or goal area to create space and opportunities to score.

> *There is only one moment in which you can arrive in time. If you're not there, you are either too early or too late.*

Johan Cruyff

Opportunity Principle

The opportunity principle might better be referred to as the *opportunist* principle. This principle recommends that any and all mistakes made by opponents should be taken advantage of, in order to be successful. Being reliant on opposition mistakes is an unreliable strategy, but the application of other concepts can encourage mistakes by the opposition.

Example

Many teams have dominated the run of a game but surrendered a positive result because of an error. At Euro 2004, England led France 1-0 until Zinedine Zidane equalized with a 90th-minute free-kick. Then, in stoppage time, Steven Gerrard attempted a back pass to David James in goal. Gerrard had not seen Thierry Henry who intercepted the pass. David James fouled Henry, conceding a penalty which Zidane duly converted.

*If you're in the penalty area and don't
know what to do with the ball,
put it in the net and we'll
discuss the options later.*

Bob Paisley

Cohesion Principle

No matter what team game is being played, 'successful' teams achieve a harmonious and cohesive relationship between all of their constituent parts. All players will be attuned to a specific objective, with a clear idea of how to achieve it through a collective structure or plan when in-possession, out-of-possession, or in transition.

The cohesion principle represents synchronization between different principles and concepts – combining to form a strategy. Game models and game cycles illustrate the principles operating in cohesion, with concepts emphasizing precisely how they play out on the field. The *ultimate* goal of the cohesion principle is to create opportunities to score, and to prevent the opposition creating opportunities to score. The details provide scaffolding to achieve this.

Cohesion can be subdivided within a team dynamic. A team is built of many smaller subsets. Partnerships form between fullbacks and wingers, central defenders, central midfielders, and forwards. Further cohesion can be formed between the units of the team – defense, midfield, and attack – with the sides (left and right) forming further subsets. Each will require an interrelated understanding to function at full potential.

*Tactics are so important because
everybody has to know what we have to
do on the pitch. The relationships and
behaviors between team-mates have to be
as good as possible.*

Pep Guardiola

Reserve Principle

Providing support to teammates will enable effective ball circulation. The reserve principle is specific to having a player available behind the line of the ball, available to pass back to when it is not possible to go forward. Offering support in deeper positions influences team shape and dispersal. Balancing ball retention and going forward allows teams to apply a measured approach to ball possession. If there is no supporting player in reserve, the team will lose possession often; too many players in support positions and possession will be strong, but penetration will be weak.

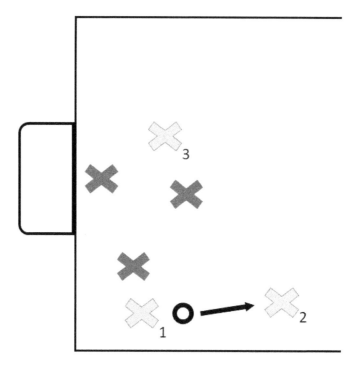

Player 2 has taken up a position behind the play, in reserve,
to support player 1, who is in possession.

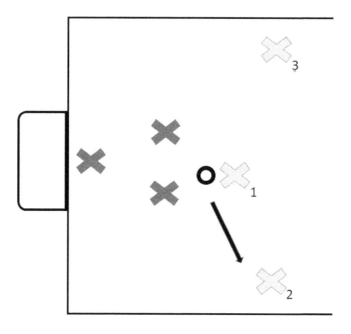

Player 2 and 3 have both taken up reserved positions to
support player 1, who is in possession.

Example

Central midfielders are often adept at offering support behind the line of the ball. Andrea Pirlo was superb at finding spaces to receive the ball, and then dictate the game. Pirlo understood that he was less likely to find space in the crowded areas ahead of the ball. Managers have also recognized that the goalkeeper is highly likely to be in a reserve position, and they can help teams retain possession.

Economy Principle

While elaborate actions excite viewers, they may not be the most efficient and economical solution to a problem. Indeed, there is an important distinction to be made between adult contexts and junior contexts. Children are in a participation or sampling context whereby they are learning about (and enjoying) the game. Many of their choices may be less economical and highly elaborate, and their choices may appear wrong because they are inefficient. However, in relation to acquiring skill over time, these choices are invaluable! When the result is truly important, the economy principle becomes more important.

 The only team that needs to win trophies is the first team. The youth teams don't need to win; they just need to make their players better.

Dennis Bergkamp

Example

Statistics tell us that most goals scored in soccer are one- and two-touch finishes inside the penalty area. This is not solely the domain of the superstar, though. In 2012, Nikica Jelavic signed for Everton and the Croatian international had a hot streak of scoring, which became notable for how many of the goals were taken with just one touch (12 of his first 15 goals for Everton). Economical finishing can also be described as clinical and cold. Single-minded forwards have just one thought… to score. When strikers are struggling for confidence in front of goal, we witness them taking extra touches by which time good opportunities have passed them by. Taking fewer touches will give the defender less time to close down the space.

Additional Alternative Principles

 A man with new ideas is a madman, until his ideas triumph.

Marcelo Bielsa

The following are potential principles of play that are alluded to in traditional principles, alternate principles, and academic principles, but not focused on specifically.

Pressure/Pressing

Thus far, pressure and pressing have featured as a part of out-of-possession and transition principles. The amount of pressure that the player in-possession is placed under will influence the game to a huge degree.

It has been identified that the relationship between the player in-possession and the closest player who is out-of-possession represents a *dyad*, comprised of a constant relationship in which the defender is looking to control the distance, while the attacker is aiming to break the relationship, to change the distances.

The distance dictates the pressure. Too far away, and the player in-possession has enough time and space to play with freedom. Too close and the defender could be over-committing. Being close might suggest heavy pressure and a challenge, but a challenge may be just what the attacking dribbler desires in order to skip away.

Pressure on the ball thwarts easy passes, dribbles, and shots; it forces mistakes and impacts decision-making. Pressure makes play predictable, and prevents time and space. The optimal distance is generally enough pressure to threaten the ball, but not allow the attacker freedom.

For the team applying pressure, the opposition's proximity to the goal they are defending plays a part. As the team in-possession get ever closer to the goal, the desired pressure will increase, with defenders aiming to prevent shots at the goal. In basketball, coaches will talk about not allowing any "uncontested shots", as a shot under no pressure is far more likely to be converted. After all, this is the concept of a penalty kick.

The purpose of pressure can be to delay those who are in possession. This can be achieved by being close enough to the ball and orientating the body in such a way that going forward is not immediately possible.

Team strategy becomes relevant at this point regarding where a team chooses to apply the pressure. Some national governing bodies promote the idea of putting the opposition under intense pressure, suggesting that pressure is applied at all times and all over the pitch. At this juncture, the concepts of pressure and pressing begin to morph together.

When executed well, pressing in the opponent's half can have the combined result of delaying the in-possession team's ability to go forward, regaining the ball, and transitioning into a counter-attack. This sounds like an ideal strategy, but there will always be trade-offs. Committing players to pressing leaves space elsewhere on the pitch which can be exploited when a press fails. Pressing and counter-pressing are not universal principles for this reason, and not all successful teams will employ pressing at all times; they will need to apply enough to pressure to the ball to prevent the opposition going forward easily (eventually regaining possession themselves).

Battle to exploit and protect space

Invasion and territory games are also spatial-temporal games. Pressure denies players space and time; movement off the ball will help players to locate the time and space they require when in-possession.

If players dominate their one versus ones, they will alter the game landscape, moving from under pressure into freshly-created space. This is just one way to find and generate space. The principles of movement – width, depth, support and positional play – are used to create space in-possession that can then be exploited in order to fashion scoring opportunities. However, these principles can also work against the in-possession team, allowing space when possession turns over.

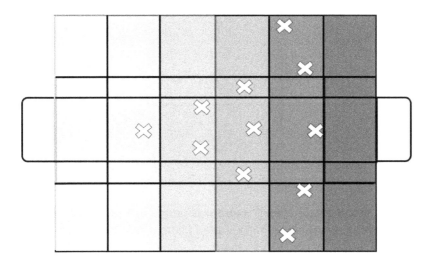

A dispersed in-possession team shape, with few central spaces that can be exploited if the ball is turned over. The three players positioned immediately in front of the two central defenders mean that layers are already in place.

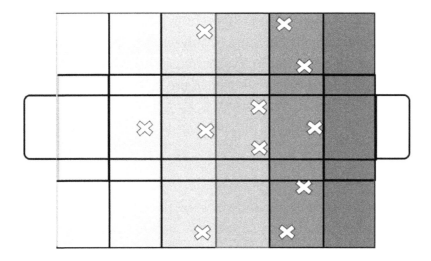

A dispersed in-possession team shape with large spaces that can be exploited if the ball is turned over. The large gaps between the defenders in the channels can be easily exploited by forwards.

77

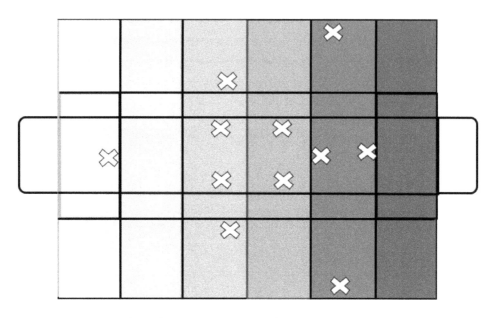

A somewhat dispersed in-possession team shape, with very few spaces that can be exploited if the ball is turned over.

Players of differing attributes will require different amounts of space to aid creation. A world-class attacker may only need a meter or two, while a young, developing soccer player might require five meters. Teams will therefore seek to limit the space available to play in, by using the out-of-possession principles. The pressure and pressing principles seek to compact the space in the immediate vicinity of the ball. German soccer has been the epicenter of high-pressure soccer in recent times. It has been common to see images of a whole team (bar the goalkeeper) concentrated within a quarter of the pitch.

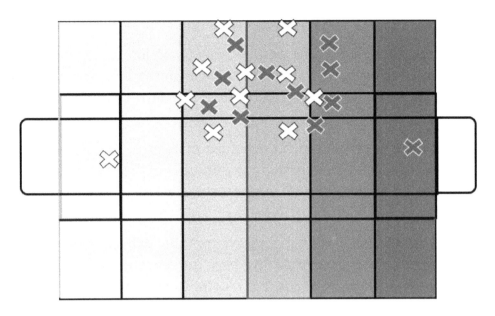

**This was witnessed in the Bundesliga game between
Bayer Leverkusen and Freiberg in 2015.**

Splitting the pitch into zones enables coaches to develop both an offensive and defensive focus in key areas. In doing so, other spaces open up – particularly behind the defensive line – but these areas can be covered by the offside law and the use of a "sweeper-keeper" who is positioned to mop up long passes into the available space.

Space can also be denied by compaction and layering, especially when prioritizing the spaces aligned centrally with the goal. The battle for time and space is most important in the areas that in-possession teams seek to penetrate into. Areas of less importance may be easier to occupy if the out-of-possession team have chosen to leave them open.

A further game concept that influences the battle for space is *marking*. Traditionally, marking is categorized as man marking or zonal marking. Nowadays, it is most common for teams to use zonal marking with some elements of man-marking. Defenders become responsible for specific areas of the pitch or specific players. The smaller the area a defending player is responsible for, the more likely it is that the in-possession player will struggle to find space. When a team moves cohesively, when out-of-possession, the zones will remain tight.

One versus one domination

In a game with equal numbers, the simplest way to exploit space (and create more space) is through one versus one domination. Systems and formations may not always lead to direct matchups but – because of the game's principles – situations will occur where players are matched up.

It is also possible for players to encourage these matchups. When players possess superior one versus one skills, the need for a number of the other principles is reduced or adjusted, particularly the support principle.

A player with superior dribbling skills can remove their immediate opponent from the equation. By eliminating that player from the defensive shape, the balance and pressure on the ball will have been broken, and another defender will have to engage the dribbler in an effort to redress the balance. In doing so, they will have to leave a space or an opponent. The dominant one versus one attacker creates space not only for themselves but for teammates.

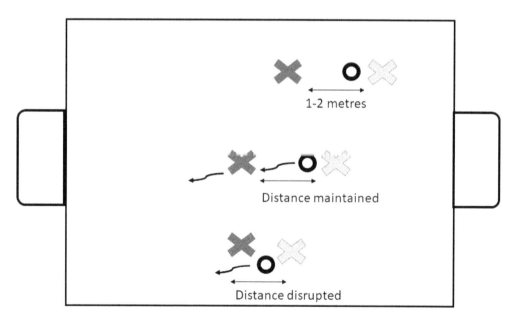

Optimum distance between attacker and defender in 1v1. By moving as the attacker moves, the defender can maintain the distance. If the attacker moves unexpectedly, the distance can be disrupted.

Players who dominate out-of-possession one versus ones, impact the principles by providing greater stability and predictability to the defending team. By reinforcing the balanced defensive structure, these players force the use of principles such as width, movement, and support to generate penetration. Defensive one versus one domination can also generate greater opportunities to create positive transitions through turnovers.

Example

Managers and coaches can make plans to negate the majority of opposition in-possession plans. What they cannot legislate for are individual mistakes or individual brilliance. The great dribblers are able to destroy tactical plans by eliminating opponents one by one and – with every opponent eliminated – they create more and more space for teammates. Like magnets, they attract opponents towards them and away from the player or space they should otherwise be marking.

Maradona's second goal against England at the 1986 World Cup has already been used as an example, but his imperious dribbling skills were also decisive against Belgium in the subsequent semi-final. Receiving the ball around 35 meters from the Belgian goal, Maradona was faced with a condensed diamond of three Belgian defenders with one further defender covering. He shifted the ball and sought the only gap between those defenders. Accelerating through the gap, he eliminated two of the initial three defenders, and the third tracked him as the covering player moved towards Maradona. This left a gap to the left of the Belgian box. A further burst of acceleration created enough space for Maradona to drill a shot into the right-hand corner of the net. Such was the acceleration required that Maradona shot off-balance; he can clearly be seen fighting to stay on his feet as he peels away in celebration. Tactical plans will always struggle to contain players who can take on half a team on their own!

Diamonds and triangles

Diamonds and triangles are such fundamental shapes in soccer that the creation of them could be considered a principle, especially when in-possession.

By forming these shapes within small zones, teams can create overloads that enable the retention of possession – thus dominating the space before moving the ball forward. The shapes create angles and passing lanes, making it possible to move the ball from one triangle or diamond into another, thus progressing and penetrating the defense with shorter spaces and through condensed spaces.

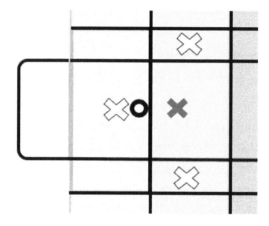

**Triangle formed between goalkeeper and
two defenders, outnumbering a lone striker.**

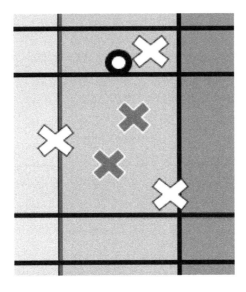

Triangle formed by three central midfielders
against two opposing midfielders.

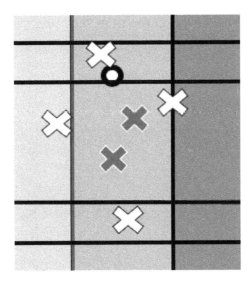

A diamond formed by four midfielders
against two opposition midfielders.

In most scenarios, it isn't the man on the ball who decides where the ball goes, but the players without the ball. Their running actions determine the next pass.

Johan Cruyff

Overloads and numerical advantage

Diamonds and triangles are examples of methods used to create a numerical advantage. These advantages can arise all over the pitch, occurring through either the deployment of players in formation or individual movement. Seeking to influence numerical sub-phases are three general principles suggested by academic researchers.

1. Do not allow a numerical advantage

2. Avoid numerical equality

3. Attempt numerical superiority

The concept that the game is won (and lost) by the team that dominates the midfield is often cited. The traditional 4-4-2 formation has fallen out of favor for this reason, as the midfield two are easily outnumbered by a midfield three derived from a 4-3-3 formation.

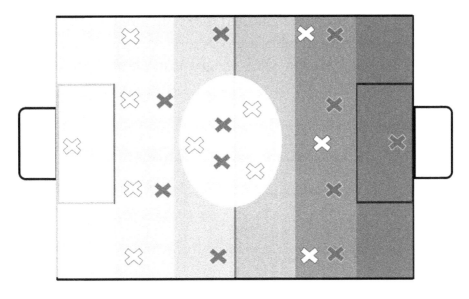

The midfield three of the white team (triangle) outnumber
the midfield pair of the dark team.

The rise of the midfield three has seen teams combat this with a midfield
diamond, outnumbering the three with a four.

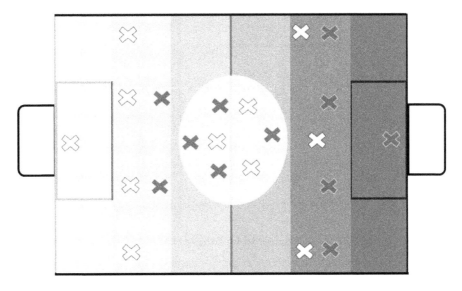

The midfield three of the white team (triangle) are outnumbered
by the midfield four of the dark team (diamond).

Teams are reluctant to counter the midfield four with a central five as this would sacrifice too many players from other areas. A more common solution to this is for the diamond to be countered with a box or square, asking questions in different zones.

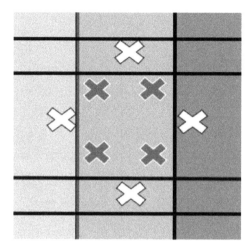

Diamond vs square (a).

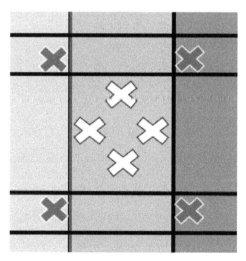

Diamond vs square (b).

It is not just in the midfield where numerical advantages can be impacted. Crucially, the number of forwards pushed directly against the opposition defensive line can dictate the shape of the game. Out-of-possession teams will not want to be outnumbered by the in-possession team's forward line, and they are highly unlikely to wish to be numerically equal; thus they will seek to have an overload in their favor.

The 4-3-3 is now the most commonly-used formation in soccer. The formation generally deploys one central striker, which allows two central defenders to outnumber the forward, giving full-backs more freedom to go forward. Should a team push two strikers against the two central defenders, the full-backs may have to stay closer to the central defenders in order to provide cover and balance.

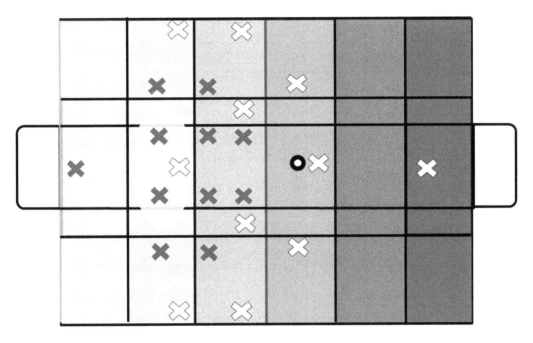

Central defenders outnumber the striker two to one (out of possession).

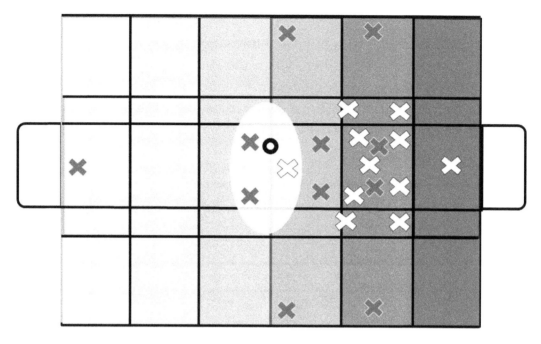

Central defenders outnumber the striker two to one (in possession).

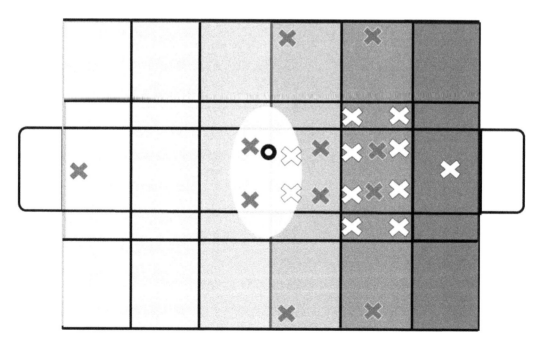

Defenders matched up two versus two against the strikers (in-possession).

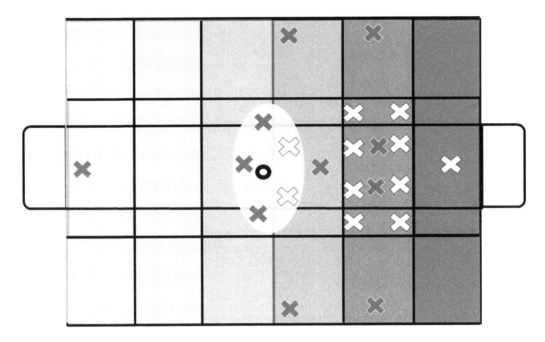

Defenders outnumber the strikers three versus two (in-possession).

The movement of the forward three can also overload the central defenders. By moving in-field, the wide players occupy the spaces between the full-backs and central defenders. The central striker can either occupy the space between the two central defenders or move away from the defenders and occupy the midfielders.

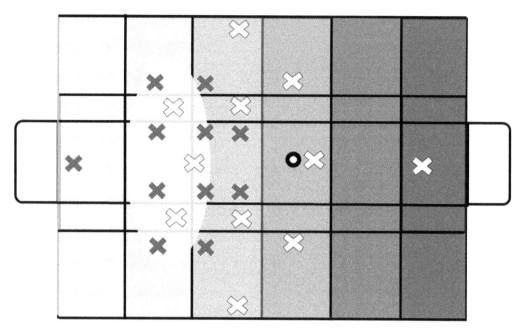

The two wingers are positioned between the full-backs and central defenders. The central striker has moved between the central midfielders. All three forwards are occupying spaces in-between, rather than placing themselves directly on a single player. These movements challenge the defenders, asking: who should be marking who?

There are many combinations of forward players possible, but the simple rule for the out-of-possession side is that however many forwards the opposition deploy, they need to have one more player in the defensive line.

In turn, width has been a recurring theme throughout the descriptions of principles and concepts. In order to utilize width, teams need players to occupy these areas. Depending on the offensive structure, players will have differing numbers of passing options. Wingers, full-backs, and wing-backs provide wide structure, but movement off the ball can also provide width. Overlaps and underlaps can create overloads, though for some a 1v1 will suffice.

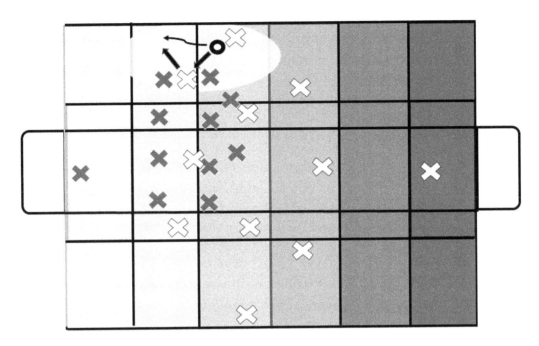

Full-back and winger combining to overlap.

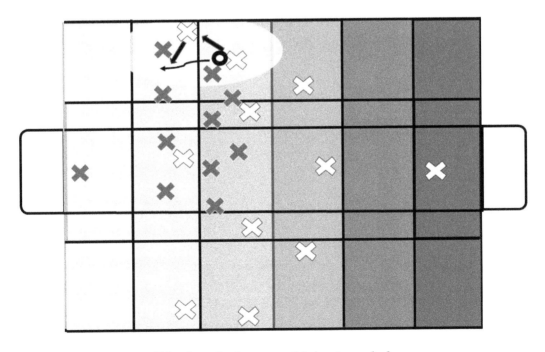

Full-back and winger combining to underlap.

Movement is significant in the creation of numerical, offensive superiority. These moments of offensive superiority may be fleeting, yet exploiting these opportunities could be crucial to winning the game. For the team out-of-possession, being able to survive moments when they are overloaded can be vital for securing victory. Thus, although being numerically superior might be useful to secure victory, it is not necessarily critical.

Example

The importance of the angles created by diamonds and triangles is so significant that certain managers and coaches will select formations that automatically create these shapes. Indeed, the Belgian FA felt them to be so significant that they utilize an 8v8 playing format in youth soccer because it creates a double diamond shape.

Carlo Ancelotti created one of the great European club midfields with a diamond shape at AC Milan. Andrea Pirlo operated at the base of the diamond, whilst Gennaro Gattuso and Clarence Seedorf performed in the two central diamond positions, both bringing different attributes to their roles. Kaka was then positioned at the top of the diamond in support of the forwards but with the freedom to roam. The diamond shape meant that the midfield was easily connected to each other with less movement required to maintain the connections. This gave Milan superiority in central areas against the majority of their opponents, not only because of additional numbers but because of superior geometry.

How The Principles Impact Practice

Soccer is a complex game. Technical, tactical, physical, psychological, and social (societal) factors warp together to influence what happens in the game. The principles are difficult to untangle from each other as they are deeply interconnected, and the same can be said for the aforementioned elements. At certain times, one aspect may be more important than the others.

For coaches, planning their focus tends to be technical, tactical *or* physical.

Understanding the principles of play will help players tactically, physically, and psychologically, but their technical skills are likely to impact their abilities to carry out the conceptual demands of the principles of play. Coaches are able to influence a player's perception of the principles by their exposure to them through practice.

This section provides example plans for the principles of play that can be used or adapted. These are just a few plans out of millions of possibilities. It should be noted that they have not been designed with a specific group of players in mind, which means that they will not meet the demands of individuals if used in the form presented.

It is important to remember that all plans are templates that should be adapted for the context they will be used in. The designs here would be suitable for adults, which may mean that they are not suitable for children without adaptation.

Penetration

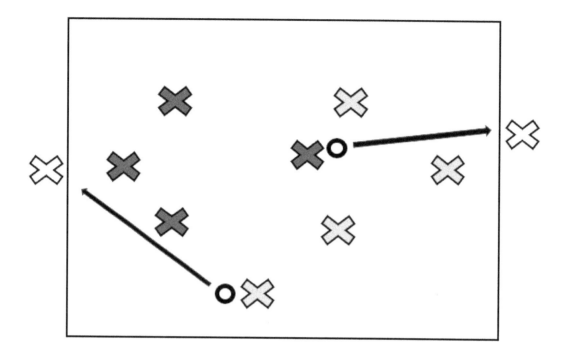

Technical practice with contextual interference.

Both teams have a ball. The white players on the end act as targets. The interior players aim to pass into the target player at one end, who will return the ball to the team who passed to them. That team will then aim to play to the other target player; thus, they will travel from end to end.

The two teams are not there to tackle each other, but the presence of an opposition provides interference to be negotiated. The act of playing into a target simulates playing forward into an attacker.

Penetration II

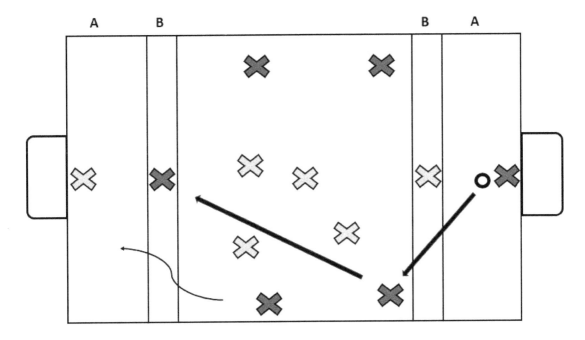

Fully opposed practice.

At each end of the pitch are *end zones* (A) that are only occupied by the goalkeeper. Ahead of that is a zone for the target man/striker (B). The objective is to play into the target man who will lay the ball off to supporting players to finish inside zone A. Defenders may mark in front of the target man but cannot enter either zone A or B *until* the ball has entered.

An alternative is for the ball to be passed into zone A for the striker to run on to. Playing into zone A immediately replicates the action of penetrating into space behind defenses.

Support

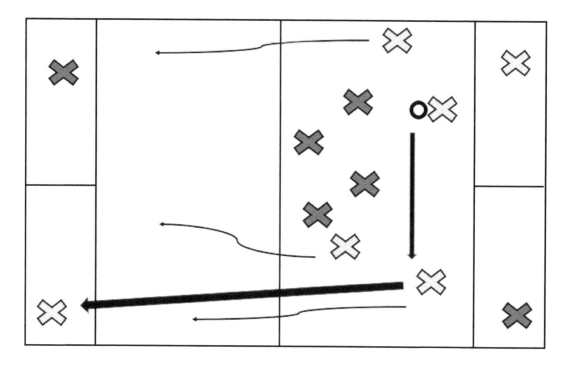

Encouraging supporting movement.

The objective of the practice is to transfer the ball from end to end. Each team has a target player in each half. When the ball is transferred, all players must switch into the half the ball has been passed into. The practice replicates players moving and reacting to the position of the ball, and seeking out new angles to support their teammates.

Support II

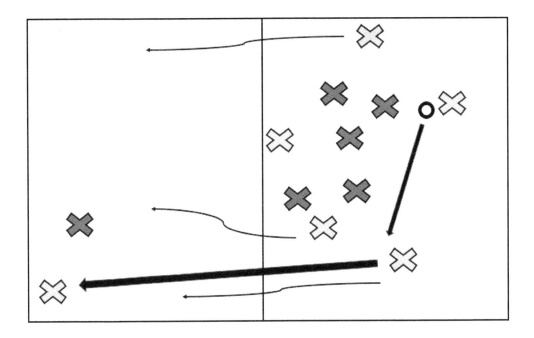

Encouraging individuals to find space.

In this version, neither team has a designated player who is locked into a zone. They must leave a single player in each half while all the other players switch. They may decide to choose a player or rotate that player, making the judgement based on observing the movement that occurs when the ball is switched. As each team has a player in the half, the receiving player will need to use movement to find space away from their potential marker.

Players will need to recognize who needs help and how they can offer that help. They will also have to recognize who is best placed to offer immediate help to the player on the ball.

Width

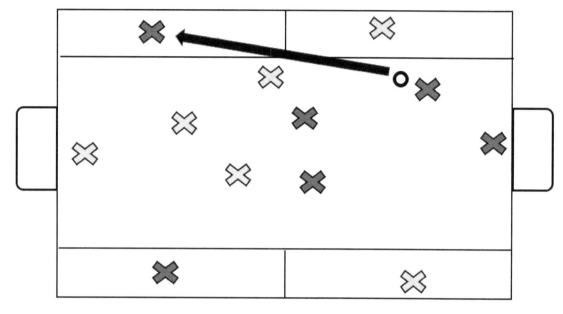

Utilizing wide zones.

Both teams have two players positioned in zones outside the pitch, in the opposition half. No defenders can enter the zones. Teams can score without using their wide players but – if they do – the goal is worth double to incentivize their use.

This set up artificially creates width by ensuring that players are positioned wide; however, the conditions should encourage players to look to pass to wide areas.

There is a possibility that the wide players will play very slowly without any defensive pressure. Should this happen, a time limit or touch limit could be applied to the wide players.

Teams may want to replicate rotation or inverted wingers driving inside. To do so, the receiving player can dribble into the central area of the pitch (or pass and follow). The player passing can switch and take up the vacated position, or that position can be taken up by the closest player.

Mobility/Movement

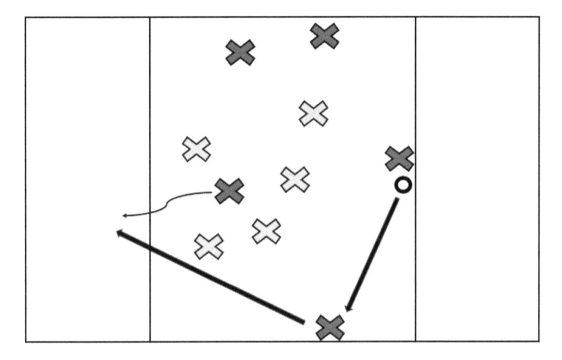

Using end-zones to simulate space behind defenders.

The grey team defend the left-hand end zone. The dark team defend the right-hand end zone. The teams score a point if they pass to a player who has made a run into the end zone to receive. Defenders are not allowed into the end zone. Under these rules, movement off the ball becomes vitally important. Players will need to recognize where the space is, and move to lose their marker.

To encourage dribbling, a point can be scored by a player who dribbles the ball into the end zone.

Improvisation/Creativity

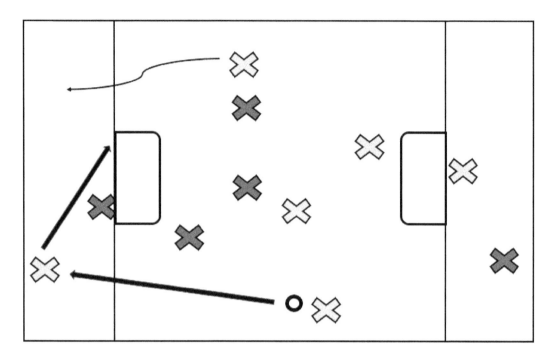

Posing players a problem that they need to solve.

The goals have been reversed and placed on the edge of the end zones. In each end zone, there is a goalkeeper and a forward. Players may enter the end zone once the ball has been passed or dribbled in. With the goals reversed, players will have to imagine different ways to create scoring opportunities through movement, support, and swift finishes. The goalkeeper may decide to position themselves in such a way that they are marking the forward, thus requiring different movement and finishes. Improvisation and creativity is also encouraged by having players in an unfamiliar environment and presenting them with a problem to solve.

Delay

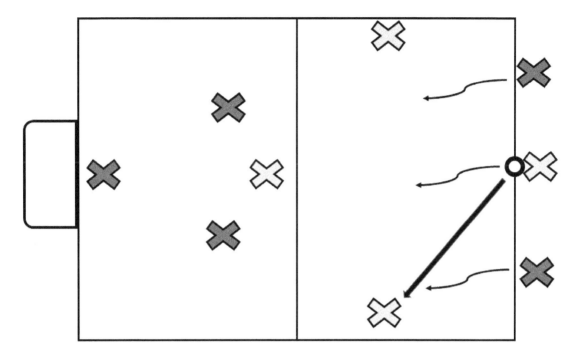

A repeated game situation.

The game is set up with three dark players in their half, one of them being the goalkeeper. A single grey player begins in that half as center-forward. In the other half are two grey players on the pitch with one grey and two dark players on the line.

The ball begins with the grey player on the line. When the grey player has passed the ball in, that player leaves the line and joins the attack to assist the grey team scoring in the goal. Meanwhile, the two dark players leave the line as soon as the receiving grey has controlled the ball, making recovery runs.

Can the two dark defenders delay the attack for long enough that the recovering players can return and reverse the overload? If the dark players regain the ball, they can score a point by crossing the end line from which play began.

Depth

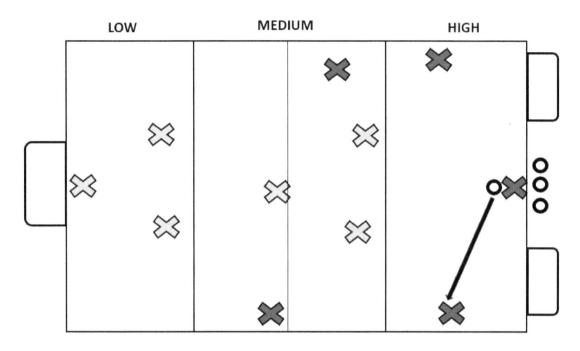

Applying the pressure zones on the pitch.

The pitch is divided into thirds with a halfway. The thirds signify different zones of pressure and depth. The halfway line is designed to help with offside.

The dark team attack with the grey team defending. For five minutes, the grey team will defend with a low point of engagement, not applying any pressure until the opposition cross the halfway with the majority of the defenders in the low zone. They will then spend five minutes with a medium point of engagement (above).

Finally, there will be five minutes with a high point of engagement with the majority of players in the high zone and no players in the low zone. Each zone will create a different picture – testing players' discipline, patience, and positioning.

Compactness

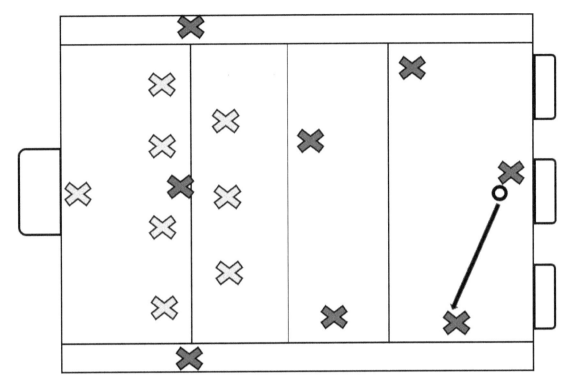

Simulating a game situation on a larger scale.

The grey team are encamped in their own half, defending the single goal. They occupy the central areas. The dark team aim to break through the low block and may use the wide areas to do so. If the grey team gain possession, they may score in any of the three mini-goals. The grey team aim to prevent the dark team from breaking through, shifting across as the ball moves and maintaining close distances between each other, making it hard to play passes through the center.

If the ball goes out to the wide areas, the grey team may send a single player (full-back) to pressure the cross. Defenders must concentrate, watching the position of the ball, the closest opponent, and their teammates. This dictates their body positions. The grey midfielders must front screen the dark striker to prevent passes in. The dark team may change their set up to include more strikers. Equally, the grey team may decide to operate with a back three and an additional midfielder.

Balance

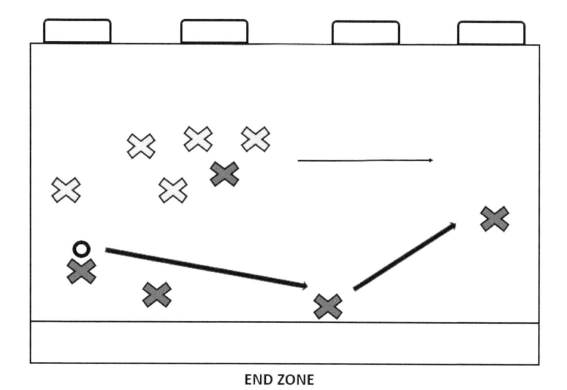

END ZONE

The pitch is wider than it is long, to challenge the defenders.

The dark team attack the four mini-goals. If the grey team regain possession, they can score by dribbling into the end zone or passing the ball to a teammate making a run into the end zone.

The grey team need to shift across with the ball to balance the backline. Their priority is to block the path of the ball to goal where the ball is positioned. The grey team leave the space furthest away from the ball as well as the player positioned furthest away from the ball and move across as the ball travels. By leaving the space, the defending team can stay compact close to the biggest threat – the ball. However, they cannot leave such a big space that it is impossible to cover the ground.

Discipline/Patience

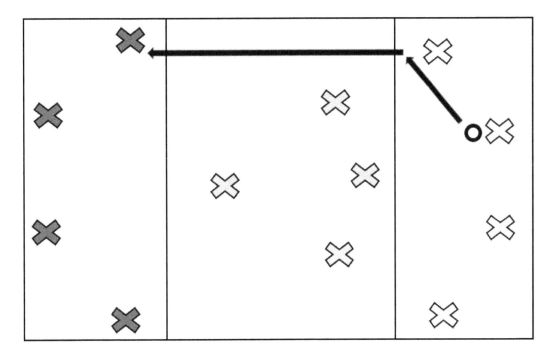

This game tests the patience of both the in-possession and out-of-possession groups.

With the area divided into thirds, the white team and the dark team aim to play across the area to each other. The grey team occupy the central zone and seek to intercept passes. The passes must be played low. If the grey team intercept, they switch with whichever team turned over possession. The grey team move across to block passes and cut passing angles. They must stay disciplined and patient, looking for the interception. The grey team will need to communicate and work together. To keep the tempo high, the team who intercept must then pass to the team who did not play the pass. For example, white passes and grey intercepts; grey then passes to dark as whites take up the position in the center and grey moves to the end position.

Counter-Attack

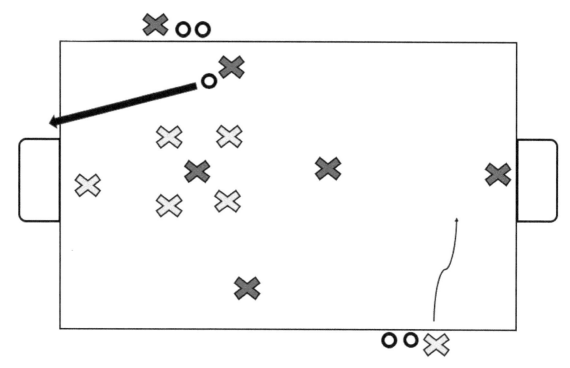

A law of soccer is changed to create a learning scenario.

Both teams have a player positioned close to the opposition goal. Whenever the ball goes out of play, the player close to the goal restarts the game. They are free to dribble or pass the ball in to restart the game.

In the situation illustrated, the dark team have taken a shot and the ball has gone out. Rather than restarting with a goal kick, the grey player can attack the goal immediately. The players' reaction to the transition needs to be quick to take advantage of the opportunity. The player who dribbles on can stay on the pitch until the ball goes out again. If it is their team's possession again, they go to the position on the side to restart.

This practice will focus more heavily on the reaction of the wide player, teammates, and the defenders, rather than any initial forward pass that begins a counter-attack.

Counter-Press

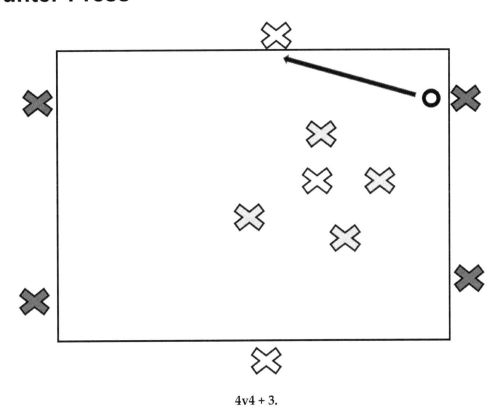

4v4 + 3.

This exercise has been made famous by Pep Guardiola and is used by many coaches. The three white players support the team in possession, and the white players at the top and bottom are free to move anywhere along their line. The white in the center may move anywhere inside the area.

The dark team are in-possession and have two players at each end. The four grey players create pressure to regain possession. Should they regain possession, the grey players take up the positions on the end, and the dark players now attempt to regain possession. The objective is for the game to be as fluid and fast as possible, but it will take large amounts of practice to get to that level.

At the transition moment, the team that loses the ball should not relax; they should pressure the ball with ferocity. Once the in-possession team have settled into position, the out-of-possession team will press with less aggression and – instead – look for triggers such as poor passes or the ball in the air. The out-of-possession team may also be able to manipulate a situation where they cut off passing lines and isolate the player in-possession, one versus two.

Possession and building out from the back

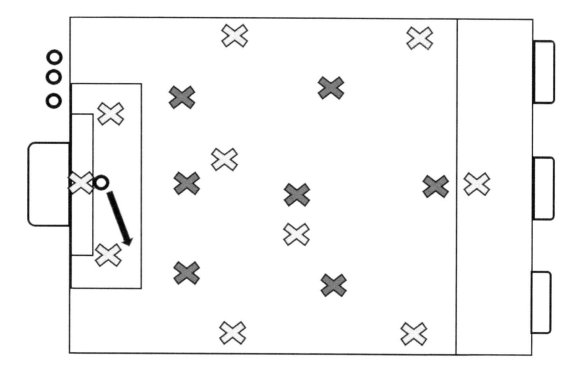

The exact positioning of players will depend on the preference of the coach.

This practice uses a little under two-thirds of a pitch. Play always starts with the grey goalkeeper with a goal kick. The grey team aim to score in any of the three mini-goals. They can only score once they have crossed the halfway line.

The dark team aim to regain possession and score in the single large goal. The goalkeeper does not have to pass short. Equally, the dark team do not have to press high. If the dark team have organized themselves with a high position, the goalkeeper may decide to chip the ball over the pressing players. In the image, this would be a three versus one in favor of the grey team. The dark team may then organize themselves further away from the penalty area, giving more space to pass the ball short. The grey team will need movement from players positioned wide and centrally to create passing lines if they are to be successful in building out from the goal kick.

Half-Spaces

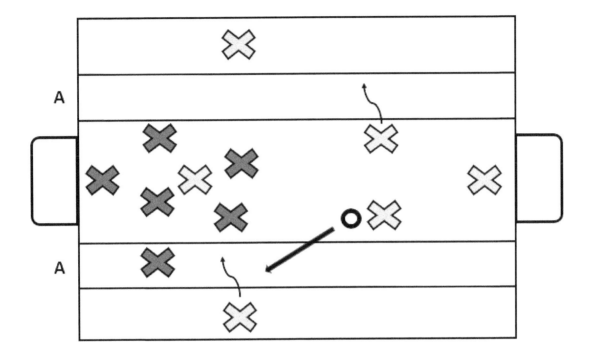

Exploiting the half-spaces through movement.

The channels marked 'A' run the length of the pitch and represent the half-spaces. No player is positioned within the half-spaces, but they can move into the half-space at any time. In this game, if an assist comes from the half-space, the goal is worth double. We can also award double if the pre-assist comes from the half-space.

Any player can occupy the half-space, but the players should be aware that if a player moves into the half-space, someone else may have to occupy the position they have left.

Showing Outside

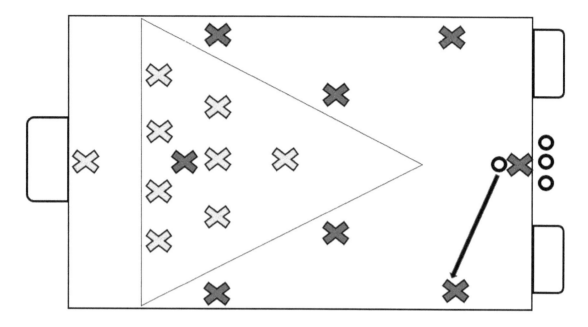

Prioritizing the middle of the pitch to protect the direct path to goal.

The grey team defend the single goal and attack the two smaller goals. The grey team also protect the area marked out with a triangle, preventing the ball from entering that area. The team will move as a unit to ensure that the gaps between players are tight enough that a pass is uninviting. This exercise will test the ability of the grey team to stay patient and maintain their shape. Should the grey team regain possession, they can spring forward to counter-attack.

Deception/Surprise

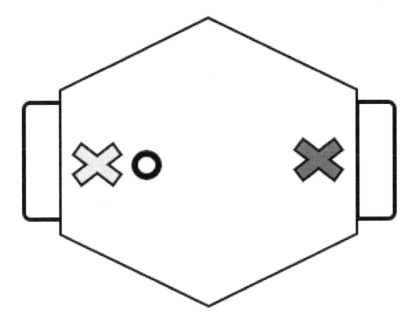

The 1v1 arena.

The game of panna (or versions of it) is superb for developing surprising individual play. In this hexagonal area, the grey player scores in the right-hand mini-goal, the dark player scores in the left-hand mini-goal. A goal is worth one point, but a nutmeg is worth five points. The participants need to manipulate, tempt, and deceive their opponent to be successful.

Deception/Surprise II

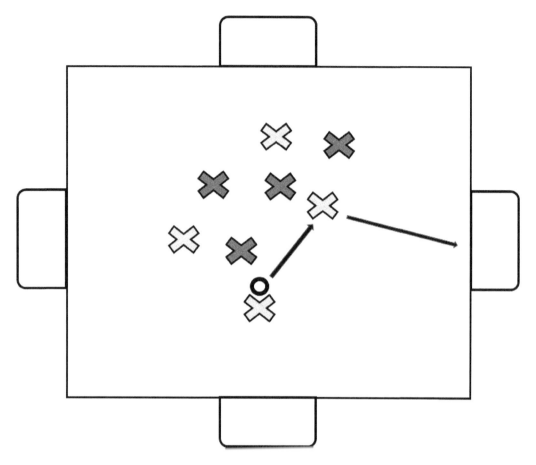

A multi-directional game.

Two teams of four playing in a game with four goals. Players can score in any of the goals. The first team to score in all four goals is the winner. Once a team has scored in a goal, they cannot score in it again. The team that concedes gets to start with the ball, playing from the goal that was just scored in. As the game is multidirectional, there are plenty of opportunities to fake and deceive the opposition; as the scoring options diminish, it becomes increasingly harder to score.

Mobility

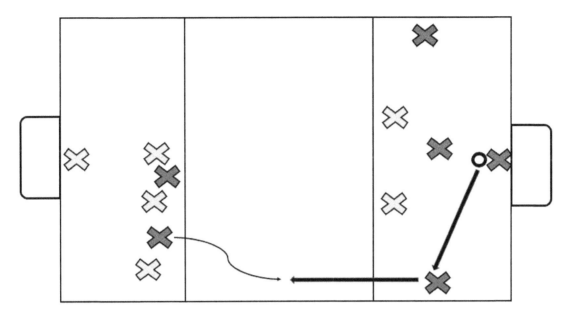

Leaving space empty so that players have to move to fill the space.

The playing area is divided into thirds. The central third is left empty while the teams have three defenders and a goalkeeper in their defending third, and two attackers in their attacking third. One of the attacking players is allowed to move into the middle third to receive. Defenders are not allowed to follow. The player who passed the ball into the central third can make an attacking run (underlap or overlap). If the goalkeeper has played the pass forward, one of the other players can make the forward run to support.

This practice replicates forwards dropping into space between the lines to receive, losing their marker; and wide players making runs to support. It is possible to switch the rules to allow a defender to step into the middle to receive.

Economy

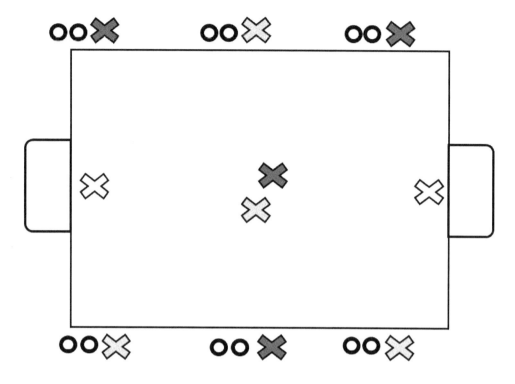

Fast-paced finishing.

The two players in the middle (one grey and one dark) play against each other. The coach decides which player starts (in this example, grey).

The grey player can receive a pass from any of his teammates. If he/she scores, they may receive another ball from any of their teammates. If the dark player gains possession, they may attempt to score. Both players can score in either goal. If the ball goes out of play (or the GK makes a save), the player who did not knock the ball out of play receives a pass from their teammate.

This game requires the attackers in the center to move intelligently to deceive their opponent. Good communication with their teammates is also required; otherwise, multiple passes may be played to the receiver simultaneously. Should the attacker create space, an economy of touches will enable them to shoot quickly, provided the first touch is orientated in such a way that allows a shot. Additional points can be awarded for a one-touch finish to encourage the action.

Reserve

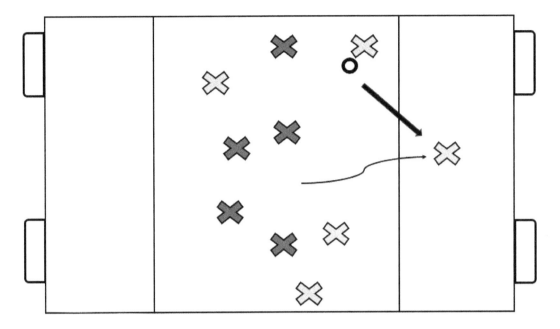

Dropping away from the play can afford a player the most space and the best perspective.

The grey team attacks the two mini goals on the left. The dark team attack the two mini goals on the right. They cannot shoot until they have entered the end zone.

When in-possession, a team's defensive end zone (e.g., the area they defend) functions as a safe zone for players to drop into and receive the ball. Alternatively, they can keep a player in the zone. This will mean that the in-possession team will always have a player in reserve to provide a passing option. Furthermore, this player will be able to survey the pitch easily, naturally orientating their body to observe the play. These positions have allowed the likes of Xabi Alonso and Andrea Pirlo to act as "quarterbacks" for their teams.

Counter-Press II

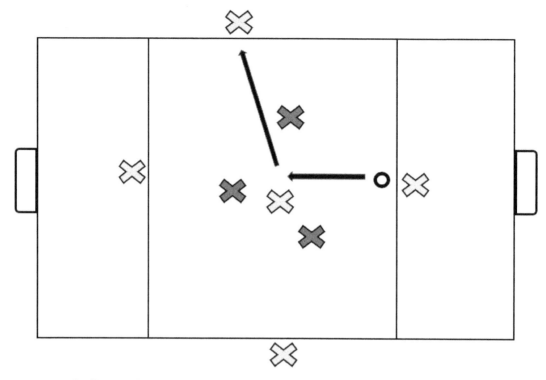

Including goals can give a realistic objective to the out-of-possession team.

The grey team are positioned around the central box with one grey on the inside, free to move within that space. There are three dark players who aim to gain possession of the ball.

The grey team score a point each time their central player receives the ball and plays out to a grey (*not* the player who just passed to them). The dark players can tackle any of the grey players and score in either of the goals. Should the grey team lose possession, they can all leave their positions to regain the ball. For the dark team, intensively pressuring the grey players on the side may not be of great benefit, but intense pressure on the central grey players will create opportunities to score. They will need to be careful in doing so to avoid being split by a pass into the central grey player. This will require them to press together and block passing lines.

Exploit and find space

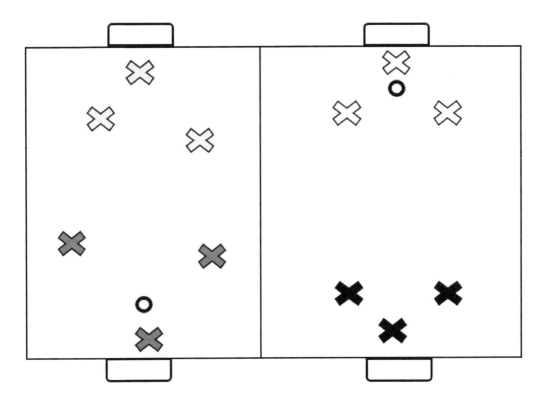

This game promotes chaos as a problem for players to solve.

Two x 'three versus three' games, playing side by side. As the game progresses, more chaos is created, and players must solve the problems created. After the initial game, the dividing line is removed, and the grey team play the black team *diagonally* across the pitch. At the same time, the white team play the dark grey team diagonally across the pitch. This will create issues of interference for players to negotiate. In the third phase, the white team and the grey team play each other while the dark grey team and the black team play each other. Having the goals on the same line creates further problems. Where will the space be, and how can they use it? Players will need to optimize their ability to observe the area and move accordingly.

One versus one domination

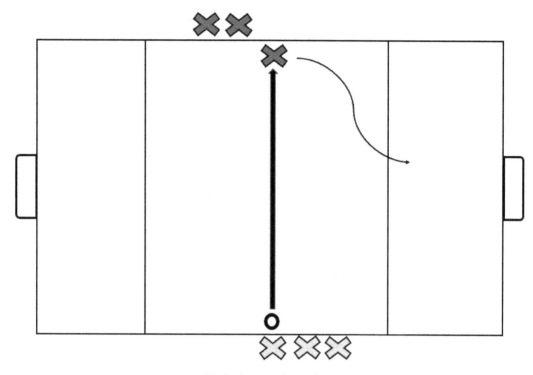

Twisting and turning.

The above practice encourages players to change direction horizontally, in a one versus one. The grey player passes to the dark player. The dark player may score in either mini goal but cannot shoot until they enter the end zone. If the grey player gains possession, they are also able to score in either mini-goal. After the attack, the players join the opposite line, switching ends.

One versus one domination II

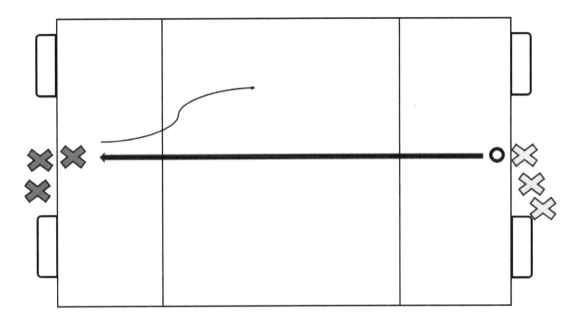

Direct dribbling.

This exercise encourages players to change direction vertically. The grey player passes across to the dark player. The player can score in either of the two mini goals at the end the grey passed from – once they have entered the end zone. If the grey player gains possession, they can score in the mini-goals behind the dark team. After the attack, the players involved swap lines.

Diamonds and triangles

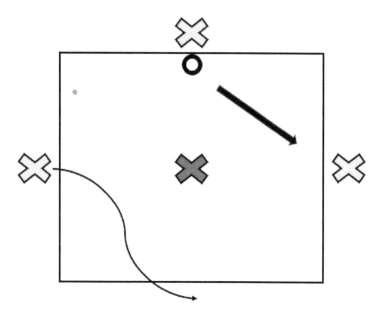

Players need to move to maintain the shape.

This exercise is designed to encourage players to move in order to create triangles. One side is deliberately left empty so that players have to recognize when to move around to fill the space. If the middle player wins the ball, they swap with whoever lost possession.

Diamonds and triangles II

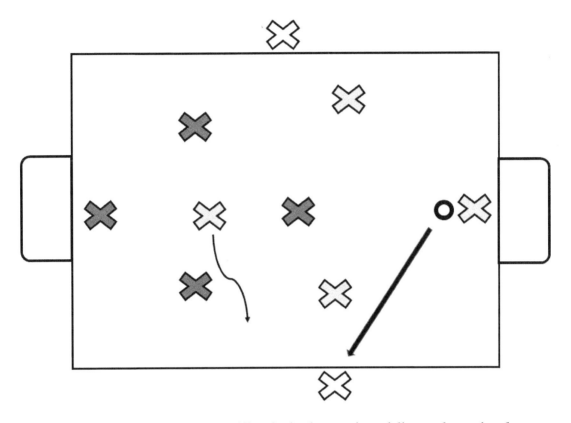

The outside players' presence will assist in the creation of diamonds or triangles.

The outside white players move along their wings to offer support to the interior players. The inside players move to support the outside players when the ball has been received. The interior players attempt to maintain diamonds and triangles in connection with themselves and the exterior players.

Create Overloads

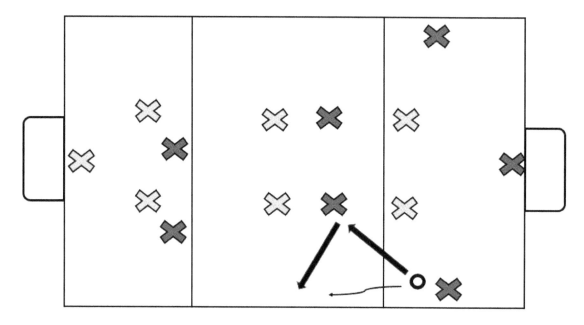

Movement will create overloads.

The pitch is divided into thirds. Each team has three players in their defensive third (including the goalkeeper): two in the midfield and two in the attack. If an outfield player from the team in-possession passes into the next zone, they can follow the pass to create an overload. Out-of-possession players are locked in their zone.

Alternatively, the players can break into the next zone with a dribble, or a player can drop into the zone where the ball is, to create the overload. Note that the goalkeeper automatically creates an overload in the defensive area when in-possession.

Conclusion

Sometimes in soccer, you have to score goals.

Thierry Henry

But only sometimes.

In possession, the only true principle is to score/create. Conversely, when out-of-possession, the only true principle is to prevent the opposition scoring/creating.

All other principles exist to scaffold these two principles. Including transition.

Positive and negative transitions are just incremental versions of in- and out-of-possession principles. True principles must be universal and inescapable, unarguable. Only scoring more than the opposition is a true indication of success in an invasion game.

It is often the effectiveness of the out-of-possession, protective concepts that require teams to delve deeper into the in-possession concepts. Highly-organized defenses, governed by the out-of-possession principles, will require creativity, deception, and surprise to break through. Poorly organized defenses – those not adhering to the out-of-possession principles – will easily be breached through the fundamental principles of economy, movement, and support.

What form the *creativity* takes may be down to individual preference or capabilities. While the belief of one coach may be that the exceptional dribbler is best placed to disorganize defenses, more commonplace in the modern game is the player with exceptional vision and technique to execute defense-splitting passes. At the highest levels, as long as victory is achieved, does the route through which success is reached matter?

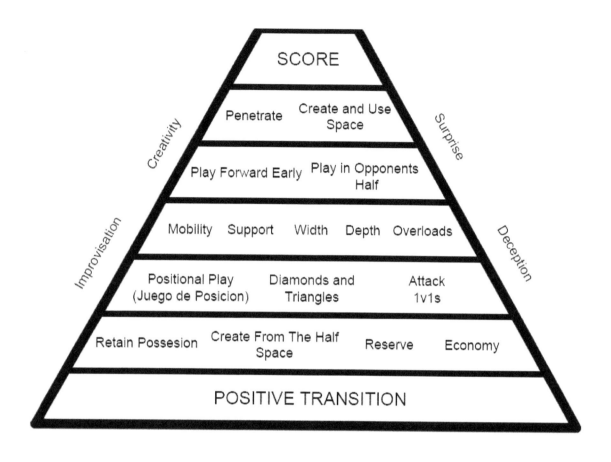

Tactically, soccer is highly logical and simple. Do the laws allow me to score from anywhere on the field? Yes. Do I have a better chance of scoring if I am positioned closer to the opposition goal? Yes. Thus, scoring is scaffolded by the concept of going forward.

Both logic and analysis indicate that being close to the goal is not enough, but certain spots offer a higher chance of scoring. These positions become more prized. An in-possession team may be able to impose their will on the out-of-possession team, but it may be more fruitful to explore the in-possession concepts until one (or some combination of concepts) affords a suitable opportunity to score.

> *In soccer, everything is complicated by the presence of an opponent.*

Jean-Paul Sartre

Some sub-principles may be more inclined towards beauty than others, but beauty itself is not a principle. If the game is about supporters and entertainment, then beauty and excitement may be taken into consideration. Entertainment may be a consideration with regard to popularity, attendance, and a "fan base" but for the majority of professional soccer clubs, teams must go beyond needing to be entertaining to achieve popularity. In fact, it is far more likely that winning will increase their popularity far more than being exciting. What of the game watched by no one? Who is there to entertain? The players and participants? For them, it may be important to be excited or engaged. Is that entertainment necessarily the same as beauty?

The concepts of a right and wrong way to play are in themselves an issue. Often, these are merely constructs built on biases, preferences, and aesthetic choices, rather than anything truly meaningful, such as context.

Soccer exists in multiple contexts beyond the elite game that we see on television or in stadiums. A huge number of adults participate in the sport, where the social aspects are more important than performance. Children and teenagers are sampling the game, learning, developing and hopefully falling in love with the sport. Victory itself becomes less crucial as we move away from the elite, and performance contexts, yet the method by which it is achieved will be linked to the principles of play, no matter what the context.

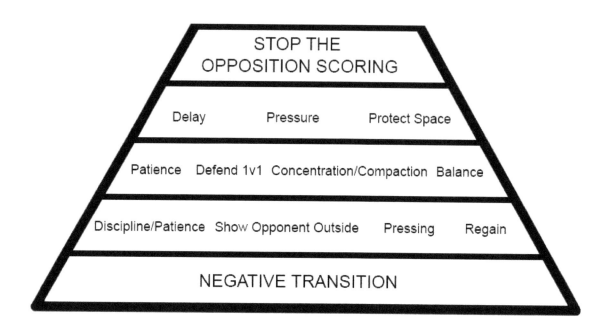

STOP THE
OPPOSITION SCORING

Delay · Pressure · Protect Space

Patience · Defend 1v1 · Concentration/Compaction · Balance

Discipline/Patience · Show Opponent Outside · Pressing · Regain

NEGATIVE TRANSITION

Debates rage around how soccer should be played. At senior levels, the game should be played to win (or at least played to achieve a desirable result) for soccer is a game with an outcome. In-possession and attacking play are more strongly associated with beauty and excitement. Defending and out-of-possession excellence are not sexy, but when the aim is to consistently achieve results, willful ignorance of out-of-possession play is perilous. Yet, the "right way" to play invariably focuses on what a team does when they have the ball. What is done without the ball is perceived as functional and effective, yet vital to team cohesion.

Regaining the ball in different areas of the pitch will have their own benefits (space behind the opponent, proximity to the opponent's goal, etc.). The immediate tariff on mistakes in certain areas will also be higher. The closer to your own goal an error is made, the greater the chance of the mistake resulting in a goal; thus, many teams have chosen to do their defensive work further from their goal in the form of high pressing. This can create a chaotic game, however, if the organization behind the press is lacking.

When in-possession, the scoring method does not matter. When defending, relying on scrambled, emergency defending is psychologically draining. If at the end of the game, the team has not conceded, then it does not matter, but the task of defending in this way for 90 minutes is extremely difficult. Being organized, with few spaces to easily exploit should mean that these emergency situations are rare, and a team can remain in control psychologically.

The principles care not for beauty. Winning cares not for beauty.

The ideas of beauty, socialization, and entertainment raise questions about the very nature of soccer itself. As a game, the objectives are clear, but as a globally, socially, and culturally significant entity, mere victory may not be sufficient to fulfil the demands placed upon soccer. Such philosophical thought will not alter the principles of play, but they will alter *the way* the principles are applied.

Coaches' and managers' actions and planning relate to the principles of play, be it tactical, technical, physical, or psychological. For young players, this can manifest as learning experiences in realistic settings. For adults, the manifestation is knowledge being utilized to gain victory. Practices will be founded around principles to either score or prevent scoring. The principles *will have* a technical impact.

In order to score, we will need to go forward, which influences the orientation of a player's first touch. Players will need the technical ability to execute passes into spaces being shrunk by compact defensive units. If teams are regularly facing packed, organized defenses, they will need to create situations that afford opportunities to create and surprise.

At the cutting edge of innovation, we witness an arms race to counteract the strategies being put in place to exploit space, or protect the space required to score. This quest to dominate and control spaces is at the very heart of soccer development. Playing between the lines and evolved midfield possession have come as a direct result of seeking space. Players drop between defensive lines to find space. The defensive midfield role has, in turn, developed to neutralize the attacker playing between the lines of defense and midfield. With this space, occupied teams have worked on the half-spaces, either side of the defensive midfielder. By applying different sub-principles, soccer remains varied. This race to exploit the principles of play will constantly develop, and the game will continue to evolve.

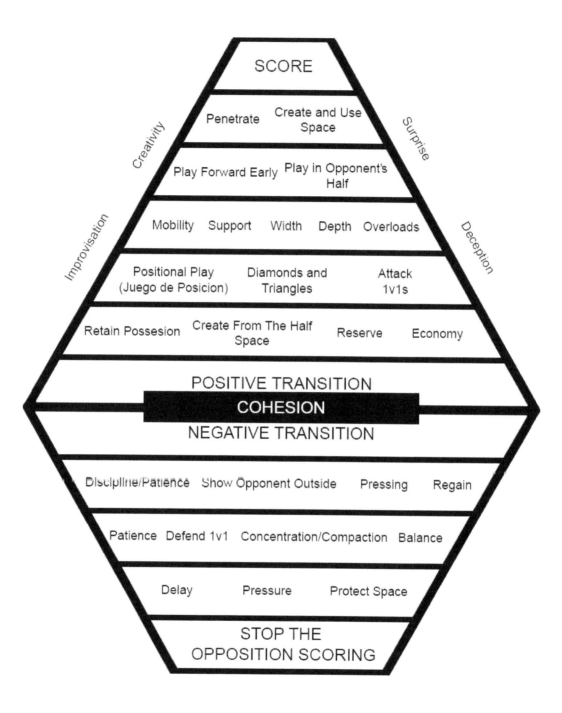

USE WIDTH DIAMONDS AND OVERLOADS
AND DEPTH TRIANGLES ATTACK 1V1
MOBILITY CREATE AND
SUPPORT USE SPACE
RESERVE CREATIVITY SUPRISE ECONOMY
POSITIONAL PLAY IMPROVISATION DECEPTION PENETRATE
CREATE FROM THE HALF SPACE
PLAY IN
RETAIN POSSESSION IN POSSESSION OPPONENT'S HALF

COHESION

NEGATIVE OUT OF POSSESION **POSITIVE**
TRANSITION **TRANSITION**

REGAIN
CONCENTRATION/COMPACTION PRESSING
SHOW OPPONENT OUTSIDE PRESSURE
BALANCE PATIENCE
DEFEND 1V1 DELAY PROTECT SPACE

Selected Sources

Bouthier, D. (1988). Les conditions cognitive de la formation d'actions sportives collectives. Nouvelle these, Université Paris: V. EPHE.

Clemente, Filipe Manuel; Lourenço Martins, Fernando Manuel; Sousa Mendes, Rui; Figueiredo, António José. A systemic overview of football game: The principles behind the game Journal of Human Sport and Exercise, vol. 9, núm. 2, abril-junio, 2014, pp. 656-667

Gréhaigne, J. F., Bouthier, D., & David, B. (1997). Dynamic-system analysis of opponent relationship in collective actions in football. Journal of Sports Sciences, 15(2), pp.137-149.

Gréhaigne, J. F., Godbout, P., & Bouthier, D. (1999) The Foundations of Tactics and Strategy in Team Sports. Journal of Teaching in Physical Education, 18, pp.159-174.

Also from Peter Prickett

Developing Skill: A Guide to 3v3 Soccer Coaching

In this book, coaches of all levels, working with players across all age groups and abilities, will learn to utilise the 3v3 method to develop skilful individuals and effective teams. The book builds up from 1v1 to 3v3 through technical exercises that improve individual skills. Then, it moves beyond 3v3, adding in more players (including goalkeepers), as situations demand it. With a core 3v3 training foundation, players will be able to explore and cement numerous key parts to their games, with depth and width, unlocking the various combinations - such as overlaps, one-twos, third-man runs, and more - which are used at all levels of the sport. At the same time, players will have ample opportunities to develop and perfect creative dribbling moves.

Developing Skill 2: A Guide to 3v3 Soccer Coaching

Peter Prickett returns with the follow-up to his 2018 3v3 bestseller with new practices that link directly into finishing and creating goals. In this sequel to *Developing Skill: A Guide to 3v3 Soccer Coaching*, the advancement of the core principles of football through small-sided games is explored further. This book's focus is on the creation and conversion of goalscoring opportunities, as well as deeper dives into session design to help coaches create better practices.

Developing Skill 2: A Guide to 3v3 Soccer Coaching outlines how you can use and incorporate the 3v3 method into your training and provides more than 85 ready-to-use, illustrated practices. It also details how best to run warm-ups, how to work with different pitch sizes and shapes, and much more.

Some of our other 25+ coaching books

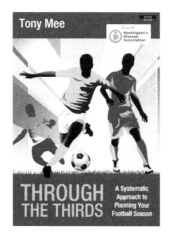

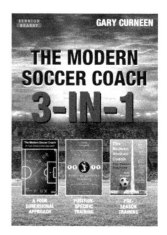

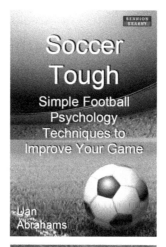

BennionKearny.com/**soccer**

CPSIA information can be obtained
at www.ICGtesting.com
Printed in the USA
BVHW010013100222
627926BV00007B/1